Second Edition

I0035594

MASS COMMUNICATION LAW IN HAWAII

By Jeffrey S. Portnoy, Peter W. Olson and Elijah Yip

NEW FORUMS PRESS INC.

Stillwater, Oklahoma U.S.A.

Printed in the United States of America.

International Standard Book Number: 1-58107-078-0

Table of Contents

About the Authors

Jeffrey S. Portnoy is a partner in the Hawaii law firm of Cades Schutte LLP. He specializes in Media and Entertainment Law and represents many television, radio, newspaper, book and magazine clients. He has been an adjunct professor in the Journalism Department at the University of Hawaii where he taught Media Law. In 1983, he received the Freedom of Information Award from the Hawaii Chapter of Sigma Delta Chi. He received his B.A. degree from Syracuse University and his J.D. degree from Duke University. He is listed in *The Best Lawyers in America* for his work in communications law.

Peter W. Olson is a partner in Cades Schutte LLP, where he has counseled and represented various newspaper, television, radio, book and magazine clients on media law matters. He has also been an adjunct professor in the Journalism Department at the University of Hawaii, teaching Media Law to undergraduate journalism students. He obtained his B.A. from the University of Notre Dame and his J.D. from The John Marshall Law School.

Elijah Yip is an associate in the litigation department of Cades Schutte LLP. He is a former law clerk to Chief Judge Emeritus Samuel P. King of the United States District Court for the District of Hawaii. He obtained his B.A. degree from the University of Hawaii at Manoa and his J.D. degree from the William S. Richardson School of Law at the University of Hawaii.

Preface

Although much of the law of mass communications is determined by federal law and federal courts interpreting our national Constitution and Bill of Rights, state legislatures and courts have significant control over many of these issues. This text is designed to serve as an overview of the law of mass communications in Hawaii. It has been written to serve students and journalists in their efforts to understand the legal requirements of a free press and free expression in this community.

The law of mass communications is constantly evolving. This book reflects the current state of the law, and future supplements will inform the reader of new developments. The end notes are not meant to be exhaustive. However, they will provide the interested reader with a wealth of additional source material.

This book reflects the collaborative efforts of several past and present colleagues at Cades Schutte LLP. Without their assistance, it would not have been possible to complete this definitive volume. Special thanks to Mark Lofstrom, as well as Donna Yamamoto, Karen Wong, Eric Young, and Jon Yoshimura for their research and comments, for their help with the original edition of this book.

I want to thank my clients who have given me the opportunity to practice in this most important area of our jurisprudence. Their devotion to their profession and their dedication to protecting our right to know is a daily inspiration. Most of all I want to thank my wife, Sandi, and my daughter, Carrie, for their support and encouragement during those times I thought I would never finish this project.

Jeffrey S. Portnoy

Chapter 1
Defamation

Hawaii's modern case law essentially follows the law of defamation outlined in the *Restatement (Second) of Torts*(1) and adopts federal case law placing constitutional limits on defamation damages(2), as set out in the seminal cases of *New York Times v. Sullivan*(3) and *Gertz v. Robert Welch, Inc.*(4)

Succinctly defined, defamation is a false communication which tends to "harm the reputation of another [so] as to lower him in the estimation of the community or deter third persons from associating or dealing with him."(5) Whether a communication has injured an individual's reputation "depends, among other factors, upon the temper of the times and the current of contemporary public opinion, with the result that words, harmless in one age, in one community, may be highly damaging to reputation at another time or in a different place."(6) Hence, the jury must determine if a statement susceptible to both an innocent and a defamatory meaning constitutes defamation.(7)

Analyzing a claim of defamation involves a four-step process:

Do the basic elements of defamation exist:

    false and defamatory language,

    damages as required by the type of statement in controversy;

    identification of the plaintiff,

    publication, and

    fault as required by the plaintiff's status?(8)

Is the plaintiff a "public" or a "private" person?

Has the defendant breached the applicable standard of conduct owed to the particular "public" or "private" plaintiff?

Are there defenses available to the defendant?

Through this process of analysis the law of defamation

attempts to balance the First Amendment guarantees of free speech and free press against the need to impose liability on those inflicting harm on others by means of defamatory falsehoods.(9)

Threshold Elements Relating to the Communication: Falsity, Defamatory Meaning and Proof of Damages, Identification, and Publication

Falsity

To be defamatory, a statement must be false *and* tend to cause injury to reputation. Publication of a false charge is presumed to be libelous subject to rebuttal that it will not tend to cause injury to reputation.(10) Falsity is usually an issue of fact to be decided by the jury.(11) In *Cabrinha v. Hilo Tribune Herald*,(12) the state supreme court distinguished false statements of fact from opinions and fair comments.(13) The plaintiff has the burden of proving falsity by clear and convincing evidence.(14)

In *Basilius v. Honolulu Publishing Co.*,(15) the federal district court in Hawaii outlined the requirements of falsity. The case involved an allegedly defamatory magazine article reporting on political and economic intrigue surrounding the 1985 assassination of Haruo Remelik, President of the Pacific Island Nation of Palau. The article reviewed various theories concerning the assassination of Remelik, including a "conspiracy theory"(16) discussed in anonymous letters sent to relatives of the former president. The letters implicated the plaintiff, a Palauan businessman, in Remelik's assassination and in efforts to secure passage of the Compact of Free Association.(17) The plaintiff argued that the article "intended to convey and did in fact convey to the community at large" that he was "in fact guilty of the crimes that the letter attributed to him."(18) Although the letters may have been defamatory and the charges in them false, the court refused to find that the article was defamatory because it did not assert or imply that the accusations in the letters were true. Because the court found that the article, read in context, accurately stated the accusations in the anonymous letters, the court held that the article was substantially true and dismissed the Complaint.

A statement that is *rhetorical hyperbole*—figurative or hyperbolic language that negates the impression that the speaker is asserting an objective fact—is not false and defamatory. In *Gold v. Harrison*,(19) ex-Beatle George Harrison, in a trial concerning a property dispute with his neighbors, was quoted by a reporter as saying, "Have you ever been raped? I'm being raped by all these people. . . . My privacy is being violated. The whole issue is my privacy."(20) The neighbors sued Harrison for defamation.(21) The court adopted the following three-part test for determining whether a statement was false and defamatory: (1) whether the general tenor of the entire work negates the impression that the defendant was asserting an objective fact; (2) whether the defendant used figurative or hyperbolic language that negates that impression; and (3) whether the statement in question is susceptible of being proved true or false.(22) Applying this standard, the court held that Harrison's statements were rhetorical hyperbole.(23)

Defamatory Meaning

An allegedly defamatory statement will fall into one of three categories that determine the recoverability of and level of proof needed to recover damages:

Communication with no defamatory meaning;

Communication which is defamatory on its face, referred to as "defamation per se"; or

Communication which can be interpreted as having both an innocent and a defamatory meaning, referred to as "defamation per quod".

If a statement does not cause injury to reputation, then no action for defamation will lie in its publication and no damages will be recoverable.(24) Actual damages need not be "limited to out-of-pocket loss [but] may, include `impairment of reputation and standing in the community, personal humiliation, and mental anguish and suffering.'"(25)

Defamation Per Se

Examples of statements considered by Hawaii courts to be defamation per se include those which:

Impute to a person the commission of a crime of moral turpitude;(26)

Have a tendency to injure a person in his office, profession, calling, or trade; or

Hold a person up to scorn and ridicule and to feelings of contempt or execration, impair him in the enjoyment of society and injure those imperfect rights of friendly intercourse and mutual benevolence which one person has with respect to others.(27)

The imputation of unfitness for particular employment, incompetence, insanity, or impairment of mental faculties are also generally held to be defamation per se.(28)

Defamation Per Quod

Defamation per quod is defamation "made by innuendo, by figure of speech, by expression of belief, by allusion, or by irony or satire."(29) If a statement's defamatory character is ambiguous, "it is for the jury to determine the sense in which it was understood."(30) Because the statement is not defamatory on its face, its libelous nature "is not obvious without an innuendo and the actionable character of such a libel depends upon a showing of special damages."(31)

In *Beamer v. Nishiki*,(32) the defendant's political ad implied that a rival candidate for lieutenant governor was a puppet of a reputed underworld figure and a union leader.(33) The ad stated: "Mehau and Trask Never Help Anyone They Don't Con-trol[.]"(34) The Hawaii Supreme Court noted that a reader could interpret "control" as "dominate" or "dictate", even though the defendant had testified that he meant "influence" (35) The court ruled that "on its face the statement f[e]ll short of being defamatory as a matter of law. It is for the jury to consider the context of the statement and determine whether it lowered [the plaintiff's] . . . reputation in the estimation of the community."(36)

Headlines may also create potential problems. In *Fernandes v. Tenbruggencate*,(37) the plaintiff, a county councilman, argued that he was defamed by a newspaper headline that read "Brother Helps in Kauai Rezoning Request".(38)

The court, however, held that the headline must be construed in conjunction with the accompanying article in order to determine whether its publication was defamatory.(39) Read as a whole, the article and headline did not suggest that the plaintiff had acted unethically.(40)

Identification

A person who claims to have been defamed must prove that he or she was the subject of the defamatory statement. This becomes an issue if the plaintiff is not directly named in the statement.

In *Cahill v. Hawaiian Paradise Park Corp.*,(41) the Hawaii Supreme Court held that the term "Cahill family" served to identify all members of the family.(42) The case arose after a radio broadcaster stated that the "entire Cahill family leans far to the left."(43) The plaintiff contended the broadcast remarks suggested, at least to some listeners, that the family members were communists or subversives engaged in activities to overthrow the government. The radio station maintained as a defense that individual members of the family could not sue because they were not mentioned by name in the broadcast. The court ruled that the statement could be reasonably construed to include each member of the Cahill family.(44)

Without specifically addressing the issue of "group libel", the Hawaii Supreme Court in *Cahill* ruled that an individual member of an identified group can maintain an action for defamation even though he or she has not been specifically named. In other jurisdictions that have directly addressed the issue of group libel, courts have stated, as a general rule, that individual members of a group consisting of less than twenty-five may bring an action for defamation while members of groups of seventy-five or more may not.(45)

Misidentification can also become an issue. In *Jenkins v. Liberty Newspaper Limited Partnership*, a newspaper misidentified an attorney as being the target of an investigation of a Maui insurance agency by the state insurance commissioner. In fact, however, it was the attorney's mother and brother who owned the agency that was under investigation. The attorney was not involved with the company in any way, except that he had represented it as its attorney in certain legal matters. The attorney sued the newspaper for defamation, asserting alternative claims based on negligence and actual malice. The Hawaii Supreme Court ruled in favor of the newspaper on both claims. With respect to the negligence claim, the court ruled that the attorney had failed to demonstrate any "actual injury", i.e., damage to his professional reputation. On the actual malice claim, the court held that attorney failed to prove with convincing clarity that the misidentification had been done purposefully or with reckless disregard of the truth. The inadvertent misidentification of the attorney, even if done negligently, did not rise to the level of actual malice.

Publication

"It is an elementary principle of tort law that defamation to be actionable requires publication. . . . [F]or [a] tort liability to lie for either slander or libel the defamation must be communicated to some third party other than the person defamed."(46) A publication is sufficient even if it is made to one person only.(47) Generally, however, where a person communicates a defamatory statement only to the person defamed, who then repeats the statement to others, the publication of the statement by the person defamed will not support a defamation action against the original maker of the statement.

A person can be held responsible for the publication of a defamatory statement even if he himself does not commit the actual act.(48) If one directs or procures the publication through a third party, publication is established in the instigator.(49) Each republication of defamatory material is a separate tort.(50) However, identifying both the source and context of the material being republished may provide a valid defense to defamation actions arising from such subsequent publication.(51)

Classifying the Allegedly Defamed Person

The second step in analyzing an action for defamation involves classifying the alleged victim as a public official, a public figure, or a private person. If the complaining party is a public official or a public figure he or she must prove that the defendant acted with actual malice. Moreover, the plaintiff must prove actual malice with convincing clarity, a higher burden of proof than the preponderance of evidence standard that normally applies in civil cases. However, if the plaintiff is a private person, a showing that the defendant acted negligently is sufficient to support a claim of defamation. In *Cahill v. Hawaiian Paradise Park Corporation*,(52) Hawaii adopted the limitations on liability imposed by such classifications of the plaintiff, as these were first set forth in *New York Times v. Sullivan*(53) and elaborated in *Gertz v. Robert Welch, Inc.*(54)

Public Officials

Hawaii courts have not yet clearly defined the term "public official". While anyone who holds elective office is a public official, not all public employees are considered public officials. Generally speaking, however, one who holds a "governmental office" may qualify as a public official.(55)

Tagawa v. Maui Publishing Co.,(56) the Hawaii case adopting the "public official" standard set out in *New York Times v. Sullivan*,(57) is an example of the application of the general rule. A news columnist criticized the use of county-owned road equipment on plaintiff Tagawa's private property.(58) The Hawaii Supreme Court ruled that because Tagawa was a member of the Maui County Board of Supervisors,(59) the actual malice standard of *New York Times v. Sullivan*(60) applied.(61) Similarly, in *Mehau v. Gannett Pacific Corp.*,(62) the court found that the plaintiffs, members of the State Board of Land and Natural Resources,(63) were public officials who had to prove actual malice on the part of the media defendant in order to prevail in their defamation suit.(64)

But government employees are not public officials in all instances. Two cases, both involving police officers, illustrate this point. In *Hoke v. Paul*,(65) a police captain alleged that the Chief of Police of the County of Hawaii prepared and published documents defaming him.(66) The court held that police captains are highly visible public officials; therefore, the actual malice standard applies to them.(67)

However, in *Aku v. Lewis*,(68) the court found that an aggrieved party, who happened to be a policeman by occupation, was not a public official for purposes of his defamation suit.(69) In *Aku*, employees of a radio station, which featured a popular personality known as "J. Akuhead Pupule," broadcast a statement that a man was fraudulently using Aku's name in order to sell fundraising tickets.(70) The Hawaii Supreme Court ruled that the plaintiff, a policeman named Earle Aku who served as coach of a community football team for which he was raising funds, was a private individual who needed only to prove negligence in order to prevail in his defamation suit.(71)

Public Figures

"[T]hose who by reason of the notoriety of their achievements or the vigor and success with which they seek the public's attention are properly classed as public figures . . . ."(72) Examples of public figures are political candidates(73) and entertainers,(74) and artists, athletes, business persons, dilettantes, or "anyone who is famous or infamous because of who he is or what he has done."(75)

In the case of *Partington v. Bugliosi*,(76) the federal district court stated that although the issue of "[w]hether, and for what purposes, a person is a p[ublic figure is a matter of law for the court to decide," "[u]nfortunately, determining precisely what individuals are public officials is an uncertain practice . . . not readily susceptible to the application of mechanical rules."(77) *Partington* afforded the federal district court an opportunity to also distinguish between general purpose public figures and limited purpose public figures. The court noted that general purpose public figures are well-known celebrities whose names are household words, reasoning that "[s]uch p[ersons knowingly relinquish their anonymity in return for fame or fortune."(78) Limited purpose public figures, on the other hand, are those individuals who inject themselves into a particular public controversy. For purposes other than their participation in that event or dispute, they are otherwise private persons.

The case involved a claim for defamation made by a Honolulu attorney, Earle Partington, who had represented Buck Walker in a criminal trial for murder on Palmyra Island, against attorney Vincent Bugliosi, who had represented Walker's co-defendant Stephanie Stearns (a.k.a. Jennifer Jenkins) in a parallel trial involving the same charges. Partington's client was ultimately convicted while Bugliosi's was acquitted. Bugliosi, already well-known for his book *Helter Skelter* based on Bugliosi's involvement in the Charles Manson trial, wrote *And the Sea Will Tell*, a book about the alleged murder by Walker and Stearns of a San Diego couple whom they had met on the isolated island of Palmyra and in whose yacht they were later spotted in Honolulu after the couple had been reported missing. Partington sued Bugliosi over passages in the book and the subsequent television docudrama that described Partington's conduct of

Walker's criminal defense in less than glowing terms.

To determine whether Partington was a limited purpose public figure, the court engaged in a two-part analysis: first, is there a public controversy?, and if so, what was the nature and extent of the individual's participation in it?(79) Though Partington was court-appointed counsel for one of the defendants in the theft and murder trials that formed the basis of the defamation suit against attorney/author Bugliosi, the court found that Partington "actively sought exposure to [sic] the media and voluntarily maintained a high profile throughout the trial. . . . Accordingly, he was a public figure for the purpose of the . . . trial."(80)

However, prominent position in a community by itself does not necessarily make a person a public figure.(81) Neither does close relationship or association with a public figure, at least by itself, make one a public figure.(82)

Private Persons

A private person is anyone who is not a public official or a public figure. In *Cahill*, the Hawaii Supreme Court recognized that the distinction is not necessarily as clearcut as it might first seem:

> Absent clear evidence of general fame or notoriety in the community, and pervasive involvement in the affairs of society, an individual should not be deemed a public personality for all aspects of his life. It is preferable to reduce the public figure question to a more meaningful context by looking into the nature and extent of an individual's participation in the particular controversy giving rise to the defamation.(83)

The distinction is based on a case-by-case examination of the "'nature and extent of an individual's participation in the particular controversy' which [may change his or her status] from private status to that of a public figure."(84) The court's holding in *Cahill*(85) illustrates that a person might be a public figure with regard to some aspects of his or her life that, by virtue of the person's participation in a public controversy or issue, place him or her in the "public vortex" and yet retain his or her status as a private person concerning other areas of his or her life.

The distinction between a public figure and a private person is important because, as previously noted, a public official or a public figure must prove that the defendant acted with actual malice in order to prevail in a defamation suit. A private person, in contrast, need only prove that the defendant acted with negligence, a lower standard of fault whose evidentiary requirements are more easily fulfilled. The different standards recognize the relatively higher ability of public officials and public figures to rebut allegedly defamatory statements through the media as well as the need, in the interest of preventing self-censorship of a free press, to tolerate publication of inadvertent falsehoods, criticisms, and arguable opinions.(86)

As the *Cahill* court's quote from *Gertz* points out,(87) the distinction between public figures and private persons applies even when a person is a public figure because he or she has placed himself or herself in a "public vortex". Whereas a person who has achieved or actively sought general fame or notoriety may be a public figure and therefore not be entitled to protection from publication absent malice of false statements about virtually any aspect of his or her life, a so-called "public vortex" public figure may claim protection as a private person when the false statements do not concern his or her involvement in the particular public controversy into which he or she has thrust himself or herself, i.e. when the statements concern private matters not related to the controversy or issue motivating public recognition of the person.(88)

Of course, if a private person does not "thrust himself into the vortex of [a] public issue, nor . . . engage the public's attention in an attempt to influence its outcome," he remains a private person for purposes of defamatory statements; involuntary connection with a public issue does not afford the media or others license without liability under the law of defamation to publish negligently made statements that can be proven to be false.(89)

Standards of Conduct

In addition to proving falsity, defamatory communication, publication, and identification, the plaintiff in a defamation suit must prove that the defendant possessed the requisite degree of fault. A private individual must prove that the defamatory statement resulted from the defendant's negligence.(90) A public figure or public official must prove that the defamatory statement resulted from the defendant's "actual malice," a term of art in defamation law.(91) A private individual seeking to recover punitive damages against a media defendant must also prove actual malice.(92) The plaintiff must prove "by clear and convincing evidence" (not simply by a preponderance of the evidence needed for most other elements of a defamation case) that the defendant has breached the relevant standard of care in publishing the alleged defamatory falsehood.(93)

The Actual Malice Test

Actual malice is defined as the deliberate falsification of the facts or the reckless disregard of the truth.(94) In Hawaii, actual malice is established if the evidence presented sufficiently shows that the defendant in fact knew that the communication was false or that the defendant entertained serious doubts as to its truth.(95) This "subjective awareness of . . . falsity"(96) can be shown by proving that "[t]here are obvious reasons to doubt the veracity of the informant or the accuracy of his reports."(97) Actual malice can also be shown by proving that a media defendant "had no reliable sources, that he misrepresented the reports of his source, or that [his] reliance upon those particular sources was reckless."(98) Reliance on normally reliable sources, such as a newswire service, will not support a finding of malice.(99)

Although the other elements in a defamation suit may be proven by a preponderance of the evidence, actual malice requires proof with clear and convincing evidence.(100) The mere existence of a defamatory statement is insufficient to support a finding of actual malice.(101) Likewise, a showing that the defendant failed to properly investigate the credibility of the alleged defamatory statement or failed to verify the accuracy of facts is not dispositive of actual malice.(102) However, a defendant cannot ensure a favorable verdict merely by professing good faith.(103)

The higher standard of proof is required of public officials and public figures in order to preserve First Amendment protection of uninhibited and robust debate on public issues.(104) Courts reason that to require a publisher or broadcaster to guarantee the truth of all factual assertions would lead to self-censorship.(105) However, the legal standard of actual malice that the plaintiff must prove in order to prevail is the same for media and nonmedia defendants;(106) the media enjoy neither broader nor more limited protection than individuals.(107)

The Negligence Test

The defendant will be judged negligent if he did not have reasonable grounds to believe that the statement was in fact true and he failed to exercise reasonable care in communicating the allegedly defamatory statement.(108)

In *Kohn v. West Hawaii Today, Inc.*,(109) the Hawaii Supreme Court examined the negligence standard as it applied to a media defendant. The defendant newspaper published an article which reported the indictment of twenty-two individuals on drug trafficking charges, identifying the drugs involved as being heroin, cocaine, hashish, and morphine.(110) The article further stated that the contraband was seized at several businesses including plaintiff's sporting goods store. In fact, police had actually only confiscated a total of six grams of marijuana from the plaintiff's store. The defendant had not checked readily available police records, which would have revealed these factual errors.(111) Nor had it following its own fact-checking procedures.

The court noted that the defendant not only "deviated from

its own standard of care" because it "had not followed the newspaper's own normal procedures in publishing the article" but also "had failed to follow [generally applicable editing and publishing] procedures normally taken to ensure accuracy."(112) The court in *Kohn* rejected defendant's argument that plaintiff was required to adduce evidence of negligence through an expert witness "who could testify about the customary practices of the news media to establish a standard of care set by the journalism profession itself."(113) The court ruled that although there may be instances where expert evidence is necessary in a private figure defamation case, the "determination of whether expert evidence is required . . . should be made on a case-by-case basis depending on the nature of the issue to be decided and the evidence actually adduced on that issue."(114) Particularly because the media defendant had failed to follow their own procedures,(115) "[t]he determination of defendant's negligence in the instant case was within the competence and understanding of laypersons. Outside expert evidence would have been unnecessary and redundant."(116)

Defenses in Defamation Actions

Truth

Truth is a complete defense to a defamation action.(117) Defamation suits are based on false statements; if the communication is true, there accordingly can be no defamation no matter how damaging the statement may be to the subject's reputation. In *Basilius v. Honolulu Publishing Co. Ltd.*,(118) the court granted summary judgment to the defendant, *Honolulu Magazine*,(119) finding that it had published an article that was "substantially true"(120) and contained "a materially accurate report of a historical fact."(121) The article concerned unresolved controversies in Palau and contained a paragraph describing an anonymous letter to relatives of Palau's assassinated president which implicated a local businessman in otherwise unsubstantiated wrongdoing. Noting that "[u]nder both federal and Hawaii law, truth is a complete defense to an action for defamation," the court explained that literal truth is not required; "[t]he proof of truth is measured by the ordinary implication of the words, i.e., the 'gist' or 'sting' of the alleged defamation."(122)

Consent

Although tort law dictates that the defense of consent may generally be raised if the defendant is prepared to prove that the plaintiff agreed to or participated in the commission of a tort,(123) i.e., the publication of defamatory statements,(124) Hawaii courts have yet to rule on the issue of consent as a defense in a defamation suit.

Opinion/Fair Comment

When a person asserts that a statement of opinion is defamatory, a publisher may assert the defense of fair comment. Hawaii state courts have yet to fully define the parameters of this defense, but in *Cabrinha v. Hilo Tribune Herald* the state supreme court noted the limitations of the defense when it stated that untrue statements cannot be protected under the guise of opinion or fair comment.(125)

In pretrial motions filed in the case of *Partington v. Bugliosi*,(126) the Hawaii federal district court discussed a defense which asserted that statements claimed to be defamatory were actually opinion. The court concluded that all but one of the contested statements about Hawaii attorney Partington made by author/attorney Bugliosi in his book *And the Sea Will Tell*, a chronicle of the widely publicized theft and murder trials of Stephanie Stearns and Buck Walker—subsequently adapted to CBS television docu-drama, were opinions and not capable of dafamatory meaning.

One contested statement not held to be opinion was the statement in the hardcover edition of the book, corrected in later editions, that "Partington was a former state prosecutor in South

Africa."(127) Partington had been a prosecutor in South Rhodesia. The court stated that:

> [W]hile it is questionable whether the statement is akin to accusing Partington of working for the Third Reich, as argued by Partington . . ., the statement is certainly capable of the defamatory meaning alleged . . . —that [Partington] "worked for and/or supported the apartheid state, system, and policies of the Republic of South Africa." Complaint at ¶ 33. The focus here is upon the nature of the inference suggested by the plaintiff. That is, whether the effect of the statement alleged by plaintiff flows reasonably from the words themselves.
>
> Here, the relationship is quite direct. The statement in question specifically implies that Partington was in some positive manner associated with the South African government. It most certainly implies that Partington worked for the South African government. In fact, it's difficult to imagine any other meaning that could naturally flow from the statement.(128)

Statements that the court found to be opinion were (1) a rhetorically posed question whether Partington had failed during the defense of Walker on the charge of murder to read the trial transcripts of the earlier-conducted theft trial(129); (2) an observation that Partington's demeanor toward the judge during the murder trial was "submissive" and analogizing the defense attorney's conduct to "steers being led to the slaughterhouse";(130) (3) comment on reasons presented by Partington for not calling as a witness a prison mate of Walker's who "had allegedly heard Walker making some incriminating statements;"(131) and (4) the narrative line in the television docu-drama that portrayed Bugliosi as saying to Stearns, "If I defend you the way Partington is defending Walker, you'll spend the rest of your life in prison."(132)

In the course of its analysis of each specific statement, the court noted that opinions are statements that could not "reasonably be interpreted as stating actual facts about an individual,"(133) statements clearly setting forth the facts upon which they rely and clearly indicating the point where the authors run out of facts and are simply expressing their own views,(134) and statements "on a matter of public concern that cannot be proven as false."(135)

Neutral Reportage

The Hawaii courts have not explicitly considered the validity of the defense called "neutral reportage".(136) The neutral reportage doctrine, established in the Second Circuit case of *Edwards v. National Audobon Society*,(137) provides qualified immunity for the reporting of verified information, even if the information reported considers only one side of an apparent controversy.(138)

However, in the *Mehau* case, the Hawaii Supreme Court held that publishers of an allegedly defamatory statement taken from the UPI newswire were shielded from potential liability by their good faith reliance on reputable news sources.(139) The Hawaii court refused to dismiss UPI, saying it could not reasonably rely on the source of its story, a controversial weekly newspaper on Maui, the *Valley Isle*. In a later decision arising out of the same case, a federal bankruptcy court held that the republication of allegedly defamatory statements by UPI was also protected by the neutral reporting defense because the statements had been independently verified by the UPI reporter.

The newswire story reported that a Hawaii paper had published an article quoting a man's view that his deceased brother belived that "Larry Mehau was the 'Godfather' of Hawaii's underworld crime."(140)

Privileged Communication

One may avoid liability for defamation by arguing that the statement was absolutely or qualifiedly privileged. Privileges arise in defamation cases when the uninhibited discussion of issues of social importance serves the public interest and is deemed necessary as a matter of public policy. "[W]hether a communication is privileged is [a matter of law] to be determined by the court."(141) A defendant enjoying an absolute privilege is absolutely immune from liability for making defamatory statements. Qualified privileges, on the other hand, protect a defendant from liability only to the extent that the privilege is not abused.

Absolute Privilege

Examples of persons who enjoy absolute privilege include participants in judicial proceedings(142) and state lawmakers acting in the exercise of their legislative functions.(143) Judges and court-appointed professionals are similarly granted absolute immunity in performing their functions.(144) Statements made by federal officials in the discharge of their duties are also absolutely privileged.(145)

In *Abercrombie v. McClung*,(146) the defendant, the newly elected president of the state senate, made an allegedly slanderous statement about a University of Hawaii faculty member, now a representative in the United States Congress, in an interview conducted in his legislative office a few hours after addressing the same issue during a speech on the floor of the state senate.(147) The court ruled that the framers of the state constitution intended to extend broader immunity to legislators(148) than they receive under the Speech and Debate Clause of the federal constitution.(149) While refusing to impose time and place restrictions,(150) the court limited the immunity to statements "made or action taken in the exercise of . . . [`legitimate'(151)] legislative functions."(152) The actual scope of the privilege, however, was left to judicial determination on a case-by-case basis. In *Abercrombie*, the court held that the state senator's statements in a press interview to clarify his speech before the legislature fell within the legislative function, even though his clarifying remarks were factually erroneous.(153) The slanderous remarks fell within an absolute privilege designed to promote "strong, fearless and responsible legislators and an informed public," the "necessary pillars of a viable democracy."(154)

Clearly, however, lawmakers do not enjoy an absolute privilege for all statements they might make. In *Mehau v. Gannett Pacific Corp.*,(155) the court found that a lawmaker's "absolute privilege" did not extend to speeches made after the close of the legislative session to an audience devoid of constituents.(156)

Qualified Privilege

A qualified privilege may arise when: [T]he author of the defamatory statement reasonably acts in the discharge of some public or private duty, legal, moral, or social, and where the publication concerns subject matter in which the author has an interest and the recipients of the publication [share] a corresponding interest or duty.(157)

To be effective, a qualified privilege must be exercised in a reasonable manner and for a proper purpose.(158) Excessive publication, use of the occasion for an improper purpose, or lack of belief or of grounds for belief that the statement made is true may indicate abuse of a qualified privilege.(159) Whether a qualified privilege has been abused is a question for the trier of fact.(160)

Persons enjoying a qualified privilege include citizens discharging some public or private duty.(161) The qualified privilege applicable to defamation cases is defined as an "interest-related" privilege; it arises because of interests shared by those making contested statements and those to whom the statements are made; and it protects those making reasonable statements in the discharge of a private or public duty—legal, moral, or social—when publication or broadcast of such statements concerns subject matter in which both the author and recipients share a common interest.(162)

The case of *Aku v. Lewis*(163) (in addition to its discussion of "public figure" status)(164) illustrates the interest-related qualified privilege and its limitations. Defendant Lewis was a popular radio personality known to listeners as "Aku". Plaintiff Aku was a football coach attempting to raise funds for his team. The fundraising consisted of a telephone solicitation campaign of 2000 households in the Kaneohe area.(165) A local TV station received two phone calls inquiring whether the radio announcer was involved in fundraising for the football team.(166) A sportscaster—learning of the calls and of radio personality Aku's disavowal of any involvement in the fundraising efforts, but without investigating further—made an on-air off-hand remark that the plaintiff was impersonating the radio figure. Lewis stated on his morning radio show that "he was the only Aku on this island and whoever was using the name Aku was a fraud."(167) The court held that Lewis' radio personality's trade name had a substantial commercial value and was a protectable interest.(168) Accordingly, Lewis was privileged to disassociate himself from the fundraising program.(169)However, the court found that Lewis had abused his qualified privilege; his accusatory statements made "went far beyond disassociation."(170) The allegation of fraud imputed criminal conduct to the plaintiff. Further, the broad publication and the method used to exercise the qualified privilege were excessive. The court pointed out that while the plaintiff's fundraising was targeted at 2000 homes in one Oahu community, the defendants had broadcast their defamatory remarks to statewide audiences.(171) Finally, the court stated that the defendants acted unreasonably in basing their belief that plaintiff was misappropriating the "Aku" trade name and de-frauding the public upon a mere two phone calls inquiring about the radio announcer's affiliation with the fundraising effort.(172)

Additional Considerations

Emotional Distress

This claim stands or falls with the defamation claim. Otherwise it would permit plaintiffs to "end run" the Constitution.(173)

Government Defendant

The State of Hawaii is immune to suits alleging defamation.(174) State employees, however, are not unconditionally immune. In *Medeiros v. Kondo*,(175) the Hawaii Supreme Court ruled that when a state official "in exercising his authority is motivated by malice, and not by an otherwise proper purpose . . ., he should not escape liability for the injuries he causes."(176)

Statute of Limitations

An action for defamation must be brought within two years or else it is time-barred under Hawaii law.(177) The period begins when the person bringing suit first learns or reasonably should have learned of publication of the disputed statements, not from the date of publication.(178) Hawaii's statute of limitations for the tort of defamation varies from that of most other jurisdictions, in which the statute of limitations usually begins to run from the date of publication.

Death

Defamation actions do not survive the death of either the plaintiff(179) or the defendant.(180)

Attorneys' Fees and Costs

As a general rule, each party bears its own attorneys' fees and costs.

Hawaii has no separate statutory scheme for awarding attorneys' fees and costs in a defamation lawsuit.

Attorneys' fees and costs may be assessed against either party if the court determines that the party's claim or defense was frivolous and not reasonably supported by the law or the facts.(181) In *Gold v. Harrison*, for example, the Hawaii Supreme Court ruled that statements made by ex-Beatle George Harrison were constitutionally protected hyperbole. As sanctions against the plaintiff for bringing a frivolous lawsuit against Harrision, the court awarded attorney's fees and costs against the plaintiff.

Endnotes

1. Restatement (Second) of Torts §§ 559 to 581A (1977).
2. Cahill v. Hawaiian Paradise Park Corp., 56 Haw 522, 535-36, 543 P.2d 1356, 1365-66 (1975) (remanding case to determine the "public figure" status of a citizen and his family allegedly defamed by a radio broadcaster's reactions to the citizen's public statements disagreeing with a speech by the Mayor of Honolulu criticizing the state judiciary's criminal sentencing standards).
3. 376 U.S. 254 (1964).
4. 418 U.S. 323 (1974).
5. Beamer v. Nishiki, 66 Haw. 572, 580, 670 P.2d 1264, 1271 (1983) (concerning political advertising implying underworld connections of a rival candidate) (citing Fernandes v. Tenbruggencate, 65 Haw. 226, 649 P.2d 1144 (1982) (quoting Restatement (Second) of Torts § 559 (1977) (citing Kahanamoku v. Advertiser, 25 Haw. 701 (1920))).
6. *Id.* (quoting Fernandes v. Tenbruggencate, 65 Haw. 226, 228, 649 P.2d 1144, 1147 (1982) (quoting Schermerhorn v. Rosenberg, 73 A.D.2d 276, 284, 426 N.Y.S. 2d 274, 282 (1980))); *see also* Kahanamoku v. Advertiser, 25 Haw. 701 (1920) (noting that social changes in the state are a factor to be considered in determining the defamatory character of a daily newspaper's sports-page commentary on swimming and surfing champion Duke Kahanamoku's failure to participate in an international competition).
7. Cahill, 56 Haw. at 527, 543 P.2d at 1361.
8. Restatement (Second) Torts § 558 (1977); *see also* Dunlea v. Dappen, 83 Hawai'i 28, 924 P.2d 196 (1996), Gold v. Harrison, 88 Hawai'i 94, 962 P.2d 353 (1998).9. Cahill, 56 Haw. at 530-31, 543 P.2d at 1362-63.
10. *Id.* at 527, 543 P.2d at 1360.
11. See id. at 529, 543 P.2d at 1362.
12. 36 Haw. 355 (1943).
13. *Id.* at 368; *see also infra* notes 121-31 and accompanying text.
14. Basilius v. Honolulu Publ'g Co., 711 F. Supp. 548, 550 (D. Haw. 1989) (citing with approval Philadelphia Newspaper, Inc. v. Hepps, 475 U.S. 767 (1986)).
15. 711 F. Supp. 548 (D. Haw. 1989).
16. *Id.* at 551.
17. *Id.* at 549.
18. *Id.* at 550.
19. Gold v. Harrison, 88 Hawai'i 94, 962 P.2d 353 (1998).
20. *Id.* at 96, 962 P.2d at 355.
21. *Id.*
22. *Id.* at 101, 962 P.2d at 360.

23. *Id.*

24. Non-defamatory statements may nevertheless be actionable under the law of torts comprising invasion of privacy, *see* ch. 2, or, depending on their source, statutory provisions designed to protect individuals' privacy and/or selected types of government functions, *see* ch. 5.

25. Cahill, 56 Haw. at 531, 543 P.2d at 1363 (quoting Gertz v. Robert Welch, Inc., 418 U.S. 323, 349, 350 (1974)).

26. Butler v. United States, 365 F. Supp. 1035, 1044 (D. Haw. 1973) (limiting defamation per se to crimes imputing "moral turpitude or a discreditable or disgraceful thing" and refusing to find libelous a letter that barred identified persons from a military base following their removal as trespassers after they had attempted to protest at a meeting between President Nixon and Japan's Premier).

27. Russell, 53 Haw. at 458, 497 P.2d at 42.

28. *Id.* at 458-59, 497 P.2d at 43.

29. Cahill v. Hawaiian Paradise Corp., 56 Haw. 522, 527-28, 543 P.2d 1356, 1361 (1975) (quoting Restatement Torts § 563 cmt. c (1938)).

30. *Id.* at 527, 543 P.2d at 1361 (citing Tagawa v. Maui Publ'g Co., 49 Haw. 675, 427 P.2d 79 (1967)).

31. Butler v. United States, 365 F. Supp. 1035, 1044 (D. Haw. 1973).

32. 66 Haw. 572, 670 P.2d 1264 (1983).

33. *See id.* at 574-77, 670 P.2d at 1267-70.

34. *See id.* at 576 illus., 543 P.2d at 1269 illus. (showing ad at issue).

35. *Id.* at 580, 543 P.2d at 272.

36. *Id.* at 581, 670 P.2d at 1272.

37. 65 Haw. 226, 649 P.2d 1144 (1982).

38. *Id.* at 227, 649 P.2d at 1146.

39. *Id.* at 230-31, 649 P.2d at 1148 (quoting Kahanamoku v. Advertiser, 25 Haw. 701, 714 (1920)).

40. *Id.* at 231, 649 P.2d at 1148; *see also* Basilius v. Honolulu Publ'g Co., 711 F. Supp. 548, 552 (D. Haw. 1989).

41. 56 Haw. 522, 543 P.2d 1356 (1975).

42. *Id.* at 528, 543 P.2d at 1361.

43. *Id.*

44. *Id.* at 529, 543 P.2d at 1361.

45. Debra T. Landis, Annotation, *Defamation of Class or Group as Actionable by Individual Member*, 52 A.L.R. 4th 618 (1990).

46. Runnels v. Okamoto, 56 Haw. 1, 525 P.2d 1125 (1974) (holding that acceptance by city council members of the truth of statements published by the city auditor regarding the management of a city facility did not create liability for defamation in the city council members) (citing William Prosser, The Law

of Torts 766 (4th ed. 1971)); *see also* Vlasaty v. Pacific Club, 4 Haw. App. 556, 560-61, 670 P.2d 827, 831 (1983) (regarding accusatory comments made by a private club's president to other employees and club members about an employee).

47. Chedester v. Stecker, 64 Haw. 464, 469, 643 P.2d 532, 535 (1982) (concerning a letter containing derogatory characterizations of a neighboring association's members sent by an association's president to a single homeowner) (citing 50 Am. Jur. 2d *Libel and Slander* § 152 (1970)).

48. *Id.*

49. *Id.*

50. Hoke v. Paul, 65 Haw. 478, 483-44, 653 P.2d 1155, 1160 (1982) (concerning a memorandum and a report distributed on different occasions to supervisory personnel and disciplinary boards).

51. *See* Basilius v. Honolulu Publ'g Co., 711 F. Supp. 548, 551-52 (D. Haw. 1989) (citing Janklow v. Newsweek, 759 F.2d 644 (8th Cir. 1985) (reporting allegedly defamatory accusations in context of their source held to be truthful)).

52. 56 Haw. 522, 543 P.2d 1356 (1975).

53. 376 U.S. 254 (1964) (requiring public officials to prove actual malice in defamation suits against media defendants).

54. 418 U.S. 323 (1974) (equating public figures and public officials for purposes of proof of fault and damages in defamation lawsuits).

55. Mehau v. Gannett Pac. Corp., 66 Haw. 133, 658 P.2d 312 (1983) (involving defamation claims by members of the State Board of Land and Natural Resources against media reporting that plaintiffs led a local crime syndicate).

56. 49 Haw. 675, 427 P.2d 79 (1967).

57. Cahill v. Hawaiian Paradise Park Corp., 56 Haw. 522, 532, 543 P.2d 1356, 1364 (1975) (listing *Tagawa* as the Hawaii case adopting the "actual malice" standard of New York Times v. Sullivan).

58. *Tagawa*, 49 Haw. at 676-77, 427 P.2d at 81.

59. *Id.* at 676, 427 P.2d at 80.

60. 376 U.S. 254 (1964).

61. *Tagawa*, 49 Haw. at 683, 427 P.2d at 84.

62. 66 Haw. 133, 658 P.2d 312 (1983).

63. *Id.* at 137, 658 P.2d at 317.

64. *Id.* at 145, 658 P.2d at 321.

65. 65 Haw. 478, 653 P.2d 1155 (1982).

66. *Id.* at 480, 653 P.2d at 1157.

67. *Id.* at 481-82, 653 P.2d at 1158.

68. 52 Haw. 366, 477 P.2d 162 (1970).

69. *Id.* at 375, 477 P.2d at 168.

70. *Id.* at 367-70, 477 P.2d at 164-65.

71. *Id.* at 375, 477 P.2d at 168. *But see* Cahill v. Hawaiian Paradise Park Corp., 56 Haw. 522, 533, 543 P.2d 1356, 1364 (1975) (suggesting that the subsequently decided case of *Gertz* permits states to interpret their constitutions to provide that when public interest issues coincide with defamation charges brought by a private person the private person plaintiff can be required to prove a higher standard of fault and that under such conditions *Aku* might have been decided differently).

72. Mehau v. Gannett Pac. Corp., 66 Haw. 133, 143, 658 P.2d 312, 320 (1983) (quoting New York Times v. Sullivan, 376 U.S. 254, 270-71 (1964)).

73. Beamer v. Nishiki, 66 Haw. 572, 670 P.2d 1264 (1983).

74. Rodriguez v. Nishiki, 65 Haw. 430, 653 P.2d 1145 (1982) (case regarding allegations of ties between organized crime and entertainers performing at political fundraising events).

75. Black's Law Dict. 1229 (6th ed. 1990) (defining "public figure" with examples as used in federal cases).

76. *See* Order Granting in Part and Denying in Part Plaintiff's Motion to Amend Complaint, Denying Plaintiff's Motion for Certification of Question of Hawaii Law and Granting in Part and Denying in Part Defendants' Motions for Summary Judgment, Civ. No. 92-00529 (June 3, 1993) (Ezra, J.).

77. *Id.* at 19-20.

78. *Id.* at 20.

79. *Id.* at 21.

80. *Id.* at 23.

81. *Cahill*, 56 Haw. at 541, 543 P.2d at 1369.

82. *Id.* at 539-42, 543 P.2d at 1367-69.

83. *Id.* at 540, 543 P.2d at 1368 (quoting Gertz v. Robert Welch, Inc., 418 U.S. 323, 352 (1974)).

84. *Id.* at 540-41, 543 P.2d at 1368 (citation omitted).

85. *Id.* at 541, 543 P.2d at 1369 (denying media defendants' motion for summary judgment absent initial proof that plaintiffs were public persons in context of the contested statements and, if so, that defendants reasonably believed that the statements made were true).

86. Gertz v. Robert Welch, Inc., 418 U.S. 323, 341 ("First Amendment requires . . . protect[ion of] some falsehood in order to protect speech that matters").

87. *See* text accompanying note 78.

88. *See, e.g., Gertz*, 418 U.S. at 352 (discussing need to reduce public-figure question to meaningful context "looking to the nature and extent of an individual's participation in the particular controversy giving rise to the defamation").

89. *Id.*

90. Mehau v. Gannett Pac. Corp., 66 Haw. 133, 143-44, 658 P.2d 312, 322 (1983).

91. Cahill v. Hawaiian Paradise Park Corp., 56 Haw. 522, 538, 543 P.2d 1356, 1367 (1975).

92. *Id.*

93. Basilius v. Honolulu Publ'g Co., 711 F. Supp. 548, 550 (D. Haw. 1989).

94. *Mehau*, 66 at 143, 658 P.2d at 320 (citing Tagawa v. Maui Publishing Co., 50 Haw. 648, 652, 448 P.2d 337, 340 (1967)).

95. Beamer v. Nishiki, 66 Haw. 572, 582, 670 P.2d 1264, 1273 (1983).

96. Gertz v. Robert Welch, Inc., 418 U.S. 323, 335 n.6 (1974).

97. DeRoburt v. Gannett Co., Inc., 507 F. Supp. 880, 883 (D. Haw. 1981) (discussing policy issues related to the challenge presented to a public figure, the President of Nauru, required to prove "actual malice" when media defendants refused to reveal their sources for allegedly defamatory reports) (quoting St. Amant v. Thompson, 390 U.S. 727, 732 (1968)).

98. *Id.* at 886.

99. Mehau v. Gannett Pac. Corp., 66 Haw. 133, 144, 658 P.2d 312, 323 (1983) (citing *Gertz*, 418 U.S. at 342).

100. Fong v. Merena, 66 Haw. 72, 74, 655 P.2d 875, 876 (1982) (refusing to find actual malice in the posting of assertedly defamatory signs concerning the voting record of a state politician running for re-election).

101. *Id.* at 75, 655 P.2d at 877.

102. *Id.* at 74, 655 P.2d at 876; Jenkins v. Liberty Newspapers, Ltd., 89 Hawai'i 254, 262-63, 971 P.2d 1089, 1097-98 (1999) (holding that reporter's failure to verify accuracy of identity of person named in a court filing prior to writing an article naming that person was insufficient to support a finding of "actual malice").

103. *See Mehau*, 66 Haw. 133, 658 P.2d 312 (1983).

104. *Id.* at 142, 658 P.2d at 319.

105. *Id.*

106. *Id.* at 143-44, 658 P.2d at 320; Rodriguez v. Nishiki, 65 Haw. 430, 437, 653 P.2d 1145, 1150 (1982).

107. *Mehau*, 66 Haw. at 143-44, 658 P.2d at 320.

108. Cahill v. Hawaiian Paradise Park Corp., 56 Haw. 522, 540-41, 543 P.2d 1356, 1368 (1975); Tagawa v. Maui Publ'g Co., 50 Haw. 648, 448 P.2d 337, 340, *cert. denied*, 396 U.S. 822 (1968).

109. 65 Haw. 584, 656 P.2d 79 (1982).

110. *Id.* at 585, 656 P.2d at 80.

111. *Id.* at 588-89, 656 P.2d at 82-83.

112. *Id.* at 588-89, 656 P.2d at 83.

113. *Id.* at 581, 656 P.2d at 81.

114. *Id.* at 589-90, 656 P.2d at 83.

115. *Id.* at 588-89, 656 P.2d at 82.

116. *Id.* at 590, 656 P.2d at 83.

117. Waterhouse v. Spreckels, 5 Haw. 246, 247 (1884) (holding that unauthorized republication of the plaintiff's letter of apology did not constitute libel when the truth of its contents had been admitted); Wright v. Hilo Tribune-Herald, Ltd., 31 Haw. 128, 131 (1929) (holding that the defendant, a newspaper that had reported that a hospital's supervisor, who had announced her resignation following a threatened investigation had taken unauthorized 'vacation' leaving all patients in the care of a single nurse, must prove the truth of the entire defamation to avail itself of the defense); Gonsalves v. Nissan Motor in Hawaii, 100 Hawaii 149, 173, 58 P.3d 1196, 1120 (2002) (rejecting defamation claim under doctrine of compelled self-publication; employer's statement that an employee was terminated for a perceived reason was truthful, regardless of whether the reason itself was accurate).

118. 711 F. Supp. 548 (D. Haw. 1989).

119. *Id.* at 552.

120. *Id.* (citing Alioto v. Cowles Comm., Inc., 623 F.2d 619 (9th Cir. 1980), *cert. denied,* 449 U.S. 1102 (1981)).

121. *Id.* (citing Janklow v. Newsweek, 759 F.2d 644, 647 (8th Cir. 1985)).

122. *Id.* at 551 (citing Kohn v. West Haw. Today, Inc., 65 Haw. 584, 590, 656 P.2d 79, 83 (1982)).

123. William L. Prosser & W. Page Keeton, Prosser & Keeton on The Law of Torts § 18 (W. Page Keeton, ed., 5th ed. (hornbook series, student ed.) 1984).

124. *Id.* § 114 at 823 (discussing consent as a defense to defamation).

125. 36 Haw. 355, 368 (1943); *cf.* Restatement (Second) of Torts §§ 606-10 (1977) (no longer requiring privilege for statements of opinion not implying a defamatory statement of fact); *see also id.* § 566 (expressions of opinion), § 580A (defamation of public official or public figure), § 580B (defamation of private person).

126. Civ. No. 92-00529 (D. Haw. 1993).

127. Order Granting in Part and Denying in Part Plaintiff's Motion to Amend Complaint, Denying Plaintiff's Motion to Amend Complaint, Denying Plaintiff's Motion for Certification of Question of Hawaii Law and Granting in Part and Denying in Part Defendants' Motion for Summary Judgment, *id.* at 10-15.

128. *Id.* at 12-13.

129. *Id.* at 24-32.

130. *Id.* at 32-36.

131. *Id.*

132. *Id.* at 41-43.

1338. *Id.* at 36.

134. *Id.* at 41.

135. *Id.* at 42 (citing federal case law).

136. Basilius v. Honolulu Publ'g Co., 711 F. Supp. 548, 552 (D. Haw. 1989) (declining to rule on validity of defense because truth or falsity was not a genuine issue of material fact in the case).

137. 556 F.2d 113 (2d Cir.), *cert. denied,* 434 U.S. 1002 (1977).

138. *In re* UPI, 106 B.R. 323, 328-30 (D.D.C. 1989).

139. Mehau v. Gannett Pacific Corp., 66 Haw. 133, 148-49, 658 P.2d 312, 322-23 (1983) (granting summary judgment to media relying on newswire releases reporting alleged defamation).

140. *Mehau,* at 148-49, 658 P.2d at 322-23.

141. Calleon v. Miyagi, 76 Hawai'i 310, 319, 876 P.2d 1278, 1287 (1994) (holding that issue of whether defamatory communication was privileged is an issue of law to be determined by the court, and that trial court erred by leaving to the jury the determination of the existence of a qualified privilege); Vlasaty v. Pacific Club, 4 Haw. App. 556, 563, 670 P.2d 827, (1983) (holding that remarks allegedly made by a private club's president to other club members and employees about an employee subsequently discharged were qualifiedly privileged as made to other employees and fellow members) (citing Kainz v. Lussier, 4 Haw. App. 400, 667 P.2d 797 (1983); Restatement (Second) Torts § 619(1) (1977)).

142. Wong v. Schorr, 51 Haw. 608, 609, 466 P.2d 441, 442 (1970) (shielding letters to Chief Justice and bar association's ethics committee that aired greivances against an attorney for his allegedly unethical conduct); Ferry v. Carlsmith, 23 Haw. 589 (1917) (shielding attorney's statements made to a jury during judicial proceedings concerning the plaintiff). *But see* McCarthy v. Yempuku, 5 Haw. App. 45, 49, 678 P.2d 11, 14 (1984) (finding attorney's defamatory statements insufficiently related to judicial proceedings to be protected by privilege) (citing Restatement (Second) of Torts § 586 (1977)).

143. Haw. Const. art. III, § 8.

144. Seibel v. Kemble, 63 Haw. 516, 525, 631 P.2d 173, 179 (1981) (refusing to allow complaint against or liability of court-appointed psychiatrists in a case alleging that negligence in diagnosis of a suspect accused of rape, sodomy, and kidnapping resulted in killing).

145. Nestor v. O'Donohoe, 429 F. Supp. 25, 28 (D. Haw. 1977) (upholding absolute immunity for military officers' evaluation reports).

146. 55 Haw. 595, 525 P.2d 594 (1974).

147. *Id.* at 596, 525 P.2d at 595.

148. *Id.* at 600, 525 P.2d at 597.

149. U.S. Const. art. I, § 6.

150. *Abercrombie,* 55 Haw. at 600, 525 P.2d at 597.

151. Haw. Const. art. III, § 8.

152. *Abercrombie,* 55 Haw. at 600, 525 P.2d at 597.

153. *Id.*
154. *Id.*
155. 66 Haw. 133, 658 P.2d 312 (1983)
156. *Id.* at 152, 658 P.2d at 324-25.
157. Aku v. Lewis, 52 Haw. 366, 371, 477 P.2d 162, 166 (1970).
158. Russell v. American Guild of Variety Artists, 53 Haw. 456, 497 P.2d 40, 44 (1972) (citing Aku v. Lewis, 52 Haw. 366, 477 P.2d 162 (1970)); Kainz v. Lussier, 4 Haw. App. 400, 405, 667 P.2d 797. 802 (1983).
159. *Kainz*, 4 Haw. App. at 405, 667 P.2d at 802.
160. Vlasaty v. Pacific Club, 4 Haw. App. 556, 564, 670 P.2d 827, 833 (1983) (citing Restatement (Second) of Torts § 619(2) (1977)); *see also* Lauer v. YMCA, 57 Haw. 390, 397, 557 P.2d 1334, 1339 (1976) (reversing trial court's decision as a matter of law that statements made by hotel manager to social worker concerning alleged misconduct of plaintiff resident were reasonable).
161. *See, e.g.*, Chow v. Alston, 2 Haw. App. 480, 484, 634 P.2d 430, 434 (1981) (holding that an allegedly defamatory memo to a superior concerning the allegedly deficient performance of a subordinate was protected by qualified privilege).
162. Aku v. Lewis, 52 Haw. 366, 477 P.2d 162 (1970); *see also Vlasaty*, 4 Haw. App. at 563, 670 P.2d at 833 (holding that supervisory staff and members shared interests with club's president sufficient to provide protection of qualified privilege for the president's statements concerning a discharged manager).
163. 52 Haw. 366, 477 P.2d 162 (1970).
164. *See* text accompanying notes 63-64.
165. *Id.* at 375, 477 at 168.
166. *Id.* at 369, 477 at 165.
167. *Id.* at 370, 477 P.2d at 165.
168. *Id.* at 371-72, 477 at 166.
169. *Id.* at 372, 477 P.2d at 166.
170. *Id.* at 372-73, 477 P.2d at 166-67.
171. *Id.* at 375, 477 P.2d at 168 (concerning "excessive publication").
172. *Id.* at 377, 477 P.2d at 169.
173. Basilius v. Honolulu Publ'g Co., 711 F. Supp. 548, 552 (D. Haw. 1989).
174. Haw. Rev. Stat. § 662-15(4) (1993 & Supp. 2002); Mitsuba Publ'g Co. v. State, 1 Haw. App. 517, 517, 620 P.2d 771, 772 (1980) (dismissing defamation claim as to state defendants).
175. 55 Haw. 499, 522 P.2d 1269 (1974) (requiring clear and convincing evidence that state tax department director acted with malice in attempts to dismiss an employee).
176. *Id.* at 503, 522 P.2d at 1271.
177. Haw. Rev. Stat. § 657-4 (1993).

178. Hoke v. Paul, 65 Haw. 478, 483-84, 653 P.2d 1155, 1159 (1982) (holding that each republication of negative reports by a police officer triggered a new limitation period) (citing Haw. Rev. Stat. § 657-7).
179. Haw. Rev. Stat. § 663-7 (1993).
180. Mitsuba Publ'g Co. v. State, 1 Haw. App. 517, 517-18, 620 P.2d 771, 772 (1980) (interpreting Haw. Rev. Stat. § 634-61 (1985) (allowing most lawsuits and causes of action to continue despite death of either the plaintiff or defendant) to exclude causes of action that are personal to the parties and dismissing defamation suit upon death of defendant).
181. Haw. Rev. Stat. § 607-14.5 (1993 & Supp. 2002).

Chapter 2
Privacy

The newest state in the Union, Hawaii is among the limited number of states adopting an explicit constitutional guarantee of individual privacy. Article I, section 6 of the Hawaii Constitution defines Hawaii citizens' right to privacy: "The right of the people to privacy is recognized and shall not be infringed without the showing of a compelling state interest. The legislature shall take affirmative steps to implement this right."(1) Hawaii's constitutional provision protecting privacy contrasts with the First Amendment, which only penumbrally provides a right to privacy.(2) Article I, section 7 of the state constitution,(3) which corresponds to federal protections embodied in the Fourth Amendment,(4) also affords limited protections against invasions of privacy.(5)

The legislature has enacted statutes regulating eavesdropping(6) and access to government records.(7) State courts have expounded on the right against invasions of privacy in cases dealing with searches and seizures(8) and defamation.(9) Nevertheless, the issue of invasion of privacy by the media has infrequently been considered in published state court decisions.

Historical Overview

In *Fergerstrom v. Hawaiian Ocean View Estates*,(10) the Hawaii Supreme Court recognized a common law cause of action for invasion of privacy under the tort of misappropriation of name and likeness for commercial purposes.(11)

The court declined to decide whether "other aspects commonly included under a general right of privacy will receive similar protection,"(12) and, to date, the state's appellate courts have reviewed no other cases specifically involving the four separate torts which comprise "invasion of privacy."

Fergerstrom involved the use, without prior consent, of the plaintiffs' names and picture in real estate sales brochures and television advertising.(13) The court held that "appropriation" of one's name or likeness for commercial purposes, without approval, is actionable under principles of tort law.(14) The court also held that recognition of such privacy rights under tort law did not interfere with constitutional rights of free speech and free press(15) explicitly protected by the First Amendment.(16)

In 1972, the legislature, in adopting the Hawaii Penal Code, a codification and amendment of the state's criminal laws based on the American Law Institute's Model Penal Code,(17) enacted a law expressly protecting privacy by making it a crime to invade another's privacy (1) by intentionally trespassing upon private property to install, (2) by installing in or near, or (3) by operating electronic surveillance equipment directed at intercepting another's communications in a private place without the consent of the person(s) entitled to privacy.(18) The law also prohibits the divulging of the contents of communications.(19) Exceptions apply to the execution of a public duty or as authorized by law.(20)

In 1978, Hawaii amended its constitution to guarantee all citizens a fundamental right to privacy.(21) This constitutional "right to privacy . . . relates to privacy in the informational and personal autonomy sense, encompassing the common law right to privacy or tort privacy, and the ability of a person to control the privacy of information about himself . . . ."(22) The constitutional right to privacy can be infringed only upon a showing of a "compelling state interest."(23)

Under federal case law, the constitutionally protected and fundamental right of privacy extends to freedom from intrusion by government upon sexual activities among unmarried heterosexual couples(24) and to autoeroticism in the home.(25) While adopting these federal precedents, the Hawaii Supreme Court has decided to go beyond other federal precedent(26) to provide that the right of privacy encompasses a right to purchase pornographic materials for use in the privacy of one's home.(27) Nevertheless, the court has not gone so far as to interpret the state constitution's privacy provision as permitting prostitution in one's home.(28) The Hawaii Supreme Court has also refused to extend the protection of privacy in one's home to permit possession of marijuana in an automobile parked in a public parking lot.(29) In general, Hawaii's constitutional right to privacy is broader than the right to privacy in the federal constitution.(30)

Article I, section 6 also requires the legislature to take affirmative steps to protect privacy rights.(31) The drafters intended that the amendment would afford protections against infringement by both government and private parties.(32) Subsequently, the legislature enacted Hawaii Revised Statutes chapter 92E governing confidentiality of personal records maintained by the government.(33) Chapter 92E was subsequently repealed and replaced by chapter 92F, the Uniform Information Practices Act (Modified).(34)

While both statutes provided protection against invasion of privacy by a government entity or use of "highly personal and intimate information" obtained from the government,(35) neither addressed exclusively private violations by private parties. The scope of protection available in Hawaii against invasion of privacy by private parties, including the media, remains largely undetermined.

Tort Law of Privacy

In addition to constitutionally based protections, the right of privacy is protected under the law of torts. The tort of invasion of privacy, which facilitates recovery against nongovernmental entities and private individuals, is actually comprised of four distinct torts, as identified in the *Restatement (Second) of Torts*.(36) The *Restatement* sets forth the American Law Institute's view of the common law of privacy, also known as "the right to be left alone."(37) This right is violated by:

(1) appropriation of another's name or likeness;

(2) unreasonable intrusions upon the seclusion of another;

(3) unreasonable publicity about another's private life; or

(4) publicity that unreasonably places the other in a false light before the public.(38)

As a general matter, however, the four traditional privacy torts are not well developed in Hawaii's case law.

Appropriation of Name or Likeness

The interest in protecting a person's name or likeness is in the nature of a property right. Accordingly, appropriation of another's name or likeness involves dual interests: an individual's personal interest in privacy and his pecuniary interest in his name and likeness.(39)

Appropriation of a person's name or likeness commonly occurs in the commercial advertising setting, as was the case in *Fergerstrom v. Hawaiian Ocean View Estates*.(40) Appropriation occurs when one takes or attempts to take for one's "own use or benefit the reputation, prestige, social or commercial standing, public interest or other values" of a person's name or likeness.(41)

Use that is merely incidental and not for a commercial purpose does not give rise to a cause of action for invasion of privacy. Neither does use for a newsworthy purpose. Both principles were argued in a Hawaii case involving the publication in the in-flight magazine of Aloha Airlines of a photograph depicting a sugar worker.(42) After the photograph had been featured in the magazine, the plaintiff filed suit alleging tortious appropriation of her likeness and seeking compensation. The court granted the airline's motion for summary judgment, noting that the use of the photograph was "merely incidental and . . . not for a commercial purpose. . . . and [that the photograph was] published in connection with a newsworthy story."(43)

An interesting privacy case concerned the unauthorized broadcast of a private videotape of celebrities Kiefer Sutherland

and Julia Roberts partying on Maui by the television show *Inside Edition*. Although Roberts and Sutherland did not pursue a claim, the owner of the videotape did. When *Inside Edition* could not demonstrate that it had permission to broadcast the tape, it paid monetary damages to settle the lawsuits.

Intrusion

Invasion of privacy under the tort of intrusion (sometimes called trespass to privacy) does not depend on publicity but on "intentional interference" with a person's interest in solitude or seclusion concerning: their person, or their private affairs.(44)

Additionally, the tort of intrusion requires intentional interference that would be "highly offensive to a reasonable person."(45)

Hawaii courts have recorded no decisions explicitly dealing with this tort. Several cases invoking the constitutional right of privacy in the context of alleged intrusions by government may give some indication as to how Hawaii courts will view potential causes of action against private individuals. Regardless, the cases illustrate the close interplay between tort law and Hawaii's constitutional guarantee, which is intended to protect individual privacy from intrusion by both governmental and private actors.

Generally, an invasion of privacy cannot occur when public places and public information are involved. A person's privacy is not invaded when another examines "public record[s] ... or documents that the [person] is required to keep and make available for public inspection."(46) This may extend to the personal financial records of a government employee bound by a constitutionally mandated code of ethics creating a government interest leading to a lowered expectation in privacy.(47)

Certain types of status, i.e., government employment,(48) may result in a person enjoying a diminished reasonable expectation of privacy. In *State v. Morris*,(49) the Hawaii Supreme Court ruled that a probationer's privacy was not invaded when he was required to submit to drug testing because, as a probationer, he had a diminished expectation of privacy regarding such matters.(50)

There is no invasion of privacy when one is not in seclusion, i.e., someone photographed walking along a public highway.(51) This is not to suggest, however, that recordation or publication of any incident or event occurring in public cannot involve an intrusion upon privacy. Interference with a person's privacy which is found to be "highly offensive" to a reasonable person or to which the "ordinary person" would "strongly object"(52) could constitute an invasion of privacy.

Even though involving a non-public location, not all intrusions upon a person's seclusion will amount to an invasion of privacy. Significantly, the *Fergerstrom* court failed to comment on this aspect of the case; the plaintiffs alleged that publication of their photograph to advertise home sales led to "a continuous stream of . . . ' sales prospects' coming on to [their] property, using [their] facilities and generally bothering [them] in their . . . home . . . ."(53)

A person's privacy may be violated by intrusions into "a private place."(54) For example, intentionally trespassing on another's property invades his privacy.(55) Place invasions can also occur when one intentionally monitors, by sight or sound, another's private affairs.(56) Accordingly, looking through another's window with binoculars or wiretapping a phone may be invasions of privacy.

In *State v. Rothman*,(57) the Hawaii Supreme Court held that under article I, section 6 of the Hawaii Constitution, "persons using telephones in . . . Hawaii [have] a reasonable expectation of privacy with respect to the telephone numbers they call on their private lines and with respect to calls made to them on their private lines."(58)

Simple investigation into another's private affairs may constitute an invasion of privacy. For example, opening another's personal mail may constitute an invasion of privacy as may a search of his or her wallet. The Hawaii Supreme Court has inferred that recording a conversation in a public restaurant constitutes an impermissible invasion of privacy if the speaker's clearly manifested behavior establishes a reasonable expectation that the conversation, even though occurring in a public location, is private.(59) However, in *State v. Klattenhoff*,(60) the Hawaii Supreme Court held that an examination of the defendant's bank account records did not constitute invasion of privacy because people do not reasonably expect that bank documents are a private matter.(61)

A compelling state interest can overcome the individual's right to privacy even if investigation is offensive to a reasonable person. In *McCloskey v. Honolulu Police Department*,(62) the Hawaii Supreme Court ruled that urinalysis drug testing of police officers comported with article I, section 6 because it was "necessary" and met the "least restrictive" alternative requirement of constitutional protection from government interference with privacy.(63)

Publicity Given to Private Life

This tort is also referred to as public disclosure of private facts. A person's privacy is invaded when the private affairs of his life are exposed and the resulting publicity:

(1) would be highly offensive to the reasonable person, and

(2) is not of legitimate public concern.

Communicating a fact about another's private life to a third party or a small group may not constitute an invasion of privacy. The requirement of publicity, as distinguished from mere publication, demands that a private matter be made known to "the public at large, or to so many people that the matter must be regarded as substantially certain to become one of public knowledge."(64)

There is no invasion of privacy if a fact is already public knowledge. Accessing public records of, for example, a person's birth certificate, record of military service, or participation in litigation does not amount to an invasion of privacy.(65) However, examination of records not open to the public, such as tax documents, may constitute an invasion of privacy.(66)

When publicity exposes embarrassing matters in a manner that would be "highly offensive to the ordinary reasonable" person, there may be an invasion of privacy, unless the private matter concerns "a legitimate public interest."(67) To constitute an invasion of privacy, a reasonable person must be justifiably distressed by the publicity given to such protected personal information.

Reports or publicity involving legitimate public concerns cannot invade privacy.(68) Often, deciding whether a private matter is of legitimate public concern requires a determination of whether the party who claims that their privacy has been invaded is a public figure. Because voluntary public figures seek publicity, they usually cannot complain of an invasion of privacy even though a fact may be damaging or unfavorable.(69) Likewise, a person who makes a public showing or participates in a public controversy to influence its outcome has no privacy right concerning matters related to the appearance or controversy.(70) Additionally, the public's legitimate interest in these types of individuals, so-called "public vortex" public figures, may reasonably extend to information about matters that would otherwise be private.(71)

Some people, although not actively seeking publicity or consenting to it, may become involuntary public figures when their conduct becomes "a legitimate subject of public interest."(72) Persons who fall into this category include those accused of committing a crime, victims of crimes or accidents, people involved in judicial proceedings, and persons involved in "other events that attract public interest."(73) At common law, although involuntary public figures may wish to avoid publicity, the public is entitled to be informed about them as a matter of legitimate public interest. Past events "may still be of legitimate interest to the public" and may be "interesting and valuable for purposes of information and education" despite the passage of even a considerable period of time.(74) However, if a person has "resumed the private, lawful and unexciting life led by the great bulk of the community," publicity about the past life which they have tried to place behind them may "utterly" ruin his or her new life.(75) Whether Hawaii's constitutional privacy provision enhances the reasonable expectation of privacy, as limited by the common law, for such involuntary public figures has not been decided by Hawaii courts.

Publicity Placing a Person in a "False Light"

Placing a person in a false light constitutes an invasion of privacy when:

the falsity would be highly offensive to a reasonable person; and the communicator, knew of the falsity, or acted in reckless disregard as to the falsity itself or the false light in which another would be placed.

False light invasions of privacy require contextually false statements, which may also give rise to actions for defamation.(76) If the matter communicated is true, there is no invasion of privacy under the tort of false light invasion of privacy. However, although many invasion of privacy actions based on false light concerns involve issues related to defamation, a cause of action for publicity in a false light need not be defamatory. It is enough if the statements, although not false in a manner that would support a claim of defamation,(77) materially misrepresent the facts.

Additionally, false light invasions require at least publication, in the legal sense of the word.(78) But, false light invasions of privacy, like claims involving unreasonable publicity, must involve more than publication and must be highly offensive to a reasonable person. The issue presented is whether the person who is the subject of the publication would be reasonably justified in feeling "seriously offended and aggrieved" by the publicity(79)—that is, by making the matters involved known to one or more third persons.

Hawaii courts have not published any decisions dealing with the tort of false light publicity. The case of *Partington v. Bugliosi* alleged defamation for statements describing the trial conduct and strategy of one attorney by the attorney for a co-defendant in a set of widely publicized theft and murder trials. The federal district court denied a motion to certify a question on Hawaii's law regarding the tort of invasion of privacy resulting from false light publicity stating that the plaintiff "has not set forth a valid claim for false light."(80)

Final Notes

Death and Privacy

At common law, the right to privacy was a personal right and most causes of action based on its tortious invasion were personal causes of action.(81) With the sole exception of appropriation of another's name or likeness, an invasion of privacy could not be claimed by anyone other than a living natural person whose privacy had allegedly been invaded.(82) Accordingly, claims based on intrusion upon seclusion, unreasonable publicity, or false light statements did not survive the death of the alleged victim.

Hawaii statutory law governing tort actions(83) provides that tort actions for "wrongful conduct, neglect, or default" may be sustained following the death of the victim except in cases involving the torts of defamation and malicious prosecution, both of which are explicitly enumerated as being exceptions to the apparently statutorily created exception to the common law.(84) Since wrongful conduct may include an unlawful invasion of one's privacy, the Hawaii statute arguably alters the common law to allow a deceased's personal representative to bring a tort action for invasion of privacy. However, the state courts have not interpreted this statute with regard to recovery by a deceased's estate for damages resulting from the tort of invasion of privacy.

Endnotes

1. Haw. Const. art. I, § 6.
2. Griswold v. Connecticut, 381 U.S. 479, 484 (1965) (guaranteeing constitutionally based protection for "zones of privacy").
3. Haw. Const. art. I, § 7 reads, in pertinent part: "The right . . . to be secure in [one's] person[], house[], papers and effects against unreasonable searches, seizures and *invasions of privacy* shall not be violated . . . ." *Id.* (emphasis added).
4. Comm. of the Whole Rep. No. 15, *reprinted in* 1 Proceedings of the Constitutional Convention of Hawaii of 1978, at 1023, 1024 (1980) (outlining that art. I, § 6 is separate and distinct from constitutional protection against unreasonable invasions of privacy in criminal investigations under art. I, § 7).
5. Jeffrey S. Portnoy, *The Lum Court and the First Amendment*, 14 U. Haw. L. Rev. 395, 418-19 (1992) (analyzing the Hawaii Supreme Court's use of Haw. Const. art. I, § 6 privacy protections to augment art. I, § 7 protections against search and seizure).
6. Haw. Rev. Stat. ch. 803, §§ 41-49 (1993 & Supp. 2002).
7. *Id.* ch. 92F (1993 & Supp. 2002); *see* ch. 5.
8. *See, e.g.*, State v. Rothman, 70 Haw. 546, 779 P.2d 1 (1989) (regarding telephone pen register); McCloskey v. Honolulu Police Dep't, 71 Haw. 568, 799 P.2d 953 (1990) (concerning drug-testing of police officer); State v. Morris, 72 Haw. 67, 806 P.2d 407 (1991) (upholding drug-testing of probationer).
9. *See* ch. 1.
10. 50 Haw. 374, 441 P.2d 141 (1968).
11. *Id.* at 378, 441 P.2d at 144.
12. *Id.*
13. *Id.* at 374, 441 P.2d at 142.
14. *Id.* at 377, 378, 441 P.2d at 143, 144.
15. *Id.* at 377-78, 441 P.2d at 144.
16. U.S. Const. amend. I; *cf.* Haw. Const. art. I, § 4 (protecting free speech and free press).
17. Haw. H.R. Conf. Comm. Rep. No. 1, 6th Leg., Reg. Sess. (1972), *reprinted in* 1972 Haw. H.R. J. 1035 (1972).
18. Act 9, 6th Leg., Reg. Sess. (1972), *reprinted in* 1972 Haw. Sess. Laws 32, 124-25 (part of provisions on public order, codified at Haw. Rev. Stat. § 711-1111 (1993) ("Violation of Privacy")).

19. *Id.* § 711-1111(1)(e).

20. *Id.* § 711-1111(1).

21. Stand. Comm. Rep. No. 69, *reprinted in* 1 Proceedings of the Constitutional Convention of Hawaii of 1978, 671, 675 (1980).

22. State v. Lester, 64 Haw. 659, 667, 649 P.2d 346, 353 (1982) (upholding undercover recordings in murder-for-hire investigations) (citing Stand. Comm. Rep. No. 69, *reprinted in* 1 Proceedings of the Constitutional Convention of Hawaii 1978, at 674-76 (1978)).

23. *See, e.g.*, State v. Kam, 69 Haw. 483, 491-92, 748 P.2d 372, 378 (1988) (upholding privacy right allowing sale and purchase of pornography for personal use in home) (citing Stand. Comm. Rep. No. 69, *reprinted in* 1 Proceedings of the Constitutional Convention of Hawaii of 1978, at 674-75 (1980)).

24. Eisenstadt v. Baird, 405 U.S. 438 (1972).

25. Stanley v. Georgia, 394 U.S. 557 (1969).

26. United States v. 12 200-Ft. Reels of Super 8Mm. Film, 413 U.S. 123 (1973) (upholding as constitutional a ban on the sale of pornographic matter for use in the privacy of the purchaser's home).

27. *Kam*, 69 Haw. at 491, 748 P.2d at 377.

28. State v. Mueller, 66 Haw. 616, 66, 671 P.2d 1351, 1358 (1983).

29. Mallan, 86 Hawai'i 440, 447, 950 P.2d 178, 185 (1998).

30. *Kam*, 69 Haw. at 491, 748 P.2d at 377; State v. Pebria, 85 Hawai'i 171, 938 P.2d 1190 (App. 1997).

31. Haw. Const. art. I, § 6.

32. Stand. Comm. Rep. No. 69, *reprinted in* 1 Proceedings of the Constitutional Convention of 1978, at 675 (1980); Comm. of the Whole Rep. No. 15, *reprinted in* 1 Proceedings of the Constitutional Convention of 1978, at 1024 (1980).

33. Haw. Rev. Stat. ch. 92E (1985) (adopted 1980, repealed 1987).

34. *Id.* ch. 92F (1993 & Supp. 2002) (Uniform Information Practices Act, adopted 1988); *see* ch. 5.

35. Painting Industry of Haw. Market Recovery Fund v. Alm, 69 Haw. 449, 453-54, 746 P.2d 79, 82 (1987) (limiting privacy protection of public records, as defined by Haw. Rev. Stat. § 92-50, to "highly personal and intimate information"); Haw. Rev. Stat. ch. 92F, pt. III (Supp. 1992) ("Disclosure of Personal Records"); *id.* § 92F-2(5) (stating that the purpose of Hawaii's Uniform Information Practices Act is to balance individuals' interest in privacy against public's interest in access to information in order to allow access "unless it would constitute a clearly unwarranted *invasion of personal privacy*" (emphasis added)).

36. Restatement (Second) of Torts § 652 (1977).

37. Samuel D. Warren & Louis D. Brandeis, *The Right to Privacy*, 4 Harv. L.

Rev. 193, 193 (1890); *see also* Olmstead v. U.S., 277 U.S. 438, 478 (1928) (Brandeis, J., dissenting).

38. Restatement (Second) of Torts § 652A(2) (1977).

39. Steven S.C. Lim, Note, *The Tort of Invasion of Privacy in Hawaii*, 1 U. Haw. L. Rev. 127, 128 n.10 (1979) (citing James M. Treece, *Commercial Exploitation of Names, Likenesses, and Personal Histories*, 51 Tex. L. Rev. 637, 653-54 (1973), and analyzing Fergerstrom v. Hawaiian Ocean View Estates, 50 Haw. 374, 441 P.2d 141 (1968)).

40. 50 Haw. 374, 441 P.2d 141 (1968).

41. Restatement (Second) of Torts § 652C cmt. c. (1977).

42. Bumacod v. Aloha Airlines, Inc., Civ. No. 88-0153 (Haw. 5th Cir. 1988).

43. *Id.*, Order Granting Defendant's Motion for Summary Judgment 2 (Jan. 26, 1989).

44. Restatement (Second) of Torts § 652B cmt. a (1977).

45. *Id.* § 652B.

46. *Id.* § 652B cmt. c.

47. Nakano v. Matayoshi, 68 Haw. 140, 706 P.2d 814 (1985).

48. *Id.*

49. 72 Haw. 67, 806 P.2d 407 (1991).

50. *Id.* at 71-72, 806 P.2d at 411.

51. Restatement (Second) of Torts § 652B cmt. c (1977).

52. *Id.* § 652B cmt. d.

53. 50 Haw. 374, 374-75, 441 P.2d 141, 142 (1968).

54. Haw. Rev. Stat. § 711-1111(1)(a) (1993).

55. *Id.*

56. *Id.* §§ 711-1111(1)(b), (c).

57. 70 Haw. 546, 779 P.2d 1 (1989).

58. *Id.* at 555-56, 779 P.2d at 7.

59. *See* State v. Okubo, 67 Haw. 197, 199, 682 P.2d 79, 80-81 (1982) (upholding plurality decision in State v. Lester, 64 Haw. 659, 649 P.2d 346 (1982) (holding consensual monitoring constitutional under art. I, § 7 protections against search and seizure)).

60. 71 Haw. 598, 801 P.2d 548 (1990).

61. *Id.* at 606, 801 P.2d at 552.

62. 71 Haw. 568, 799 P.2d 953 (1990).

63. *Id.* at 577, 799 P.2d at 958.

64. Restatement (Second) of Torts § 652D cmt. a (1977).

65. Haw. Rev. Stat. § 92F-14 (1993 & Supp. 2002).

66. Restatement (Second) of Torts § 652D cmt. b (1977); Haw. Rev. Stat. §§ 92F-13(1), 92F-14 (1993 & Supp. 2002) (exempting from disclosure government records whose disclosure "would constitute a clearly unwarranted invasion of personal privacy" and defining such invasions with examples of

information in which individuals maintain significant privacy interests); *see infra* ch. 5.

67. Restatement (Second) of Torts § 652D cmt. c (1977); Haw. Rev. Stat. § 92F-14(a) (1993 & Supp. 2002) ("Disclosure of a government record shall not constitute a clearly unwarranted invasion of personal privacy if the public interest in disclosure outweighs the privacy interests of the individual.").

68. Haw. Rev. Stat. § 92F-14(a) (1993 & Supp. 2002); *see also* SHOPO v. Society of Prof'l Journalists—Univ. of Haw. Chapter, 83 Hawai'i 378, 399, 927 P.2d 386, 407 (1996) (holding that information that must be disclosed pursuant to Hawaii's Uniform Information Practices Act regarding a public employee's employment-related misconduct is not "highly personal and intimate information" and, therefore, is not within scope of Hawaii's constitutional right to privacy).

69. *See* Mehau v. Gannett Pac. Corp., 66 Haw. 133, 143, 658 P.2d 312, 320 (1983) (holding that "public figure" status of state board members gained by virtue of "notoriety of achievements" or "vigor and success" in seeking public attention would require proof of actual malice in defamation action).

70. *See* Cahill v. Hawaiian Paradise Park Corp., 56 Haw. 522, 540, 543 P.2d 1356, 1368 (1975) (limiting public figure classification to public appearance and participation) (quoting Gertz v. Robert Welch, Inc., 418 U.S. 323, 342 (1974)).

71. Restatement (Second) of Torts § 652D cmt. e (1977); Nakano v. Matayoshi, 68 Haw. 140, 148, 706 P.2d 814, 819 (1985) (holding that constitutional protection of privacy is balanced by constitutional requirement that state and local governments adopt and enforce codes of ethics applying to their employees).

72. Restatement (Second) of Torts § 652D cmt. f (1977).

73. *Id.*

74. *Id.*

75. *Id.*

76. *See* ch. 1.

77. *See* ch. 1; Steven S.C. Lim, Note, *The Tort of Invasion of Privacy in Hawaii*, 1 U. Haw. L. Rev. 127, 133 (1979).

78. Black's Law Dict. 1227 (6th ed. 1991) (defining "publication" as "both a business term meaning printing and distribution of written materials and a legal term meaning communication of libelous matter to a third person").

79. Restatement (Second) of Torts § 652E cmt. c (1977).

80. Order Granting in Part and Denying in Part Plaintiff's Motion to Amend Complaint, Denying Plaintiff's Motion for Certification of Question of Hawaii Law and Granting in Part and Denying in Part Defendants' Motions for Summary Judgment 44, Partington v. Bugliosi, Civ. No. 92-00529 (D. Haw. June 3, 1993).

81. *See* Mitsuba Publ'g Co. v. State, 1 Haw. App. 517, 620 P.2d 771 (1980) (dismissing defamation action upon death of defendant).

82. Restatement (Second) of Torts § 652I (1977).

83. Haw. Rev. Stat. ch. 663 (1993 & Supp. 2002).

84. *Id.* § 663-7.

Chapter 3
Obscenity

In its definition of pornography, the Hawaii law on obscenity generally follows the United States Supreme Court's *Miller*(1) standard. However, while proscription of obscenity under federal law is limited by the penumbrally defined right of privacy found in the United States Constitution,(2) regulation of obscenity under Hawaii law must accommodate the explicit constitutional guarantee of privacy contained in the Hawaii Constitution.(3) As might be expected then, regulation of obscenity under Hawaii law is less restrictive than under federal law.(4) Hawaii law not only affords individuals the right to view pornographic material privately(5) but also a correlative right to purchase such materials for personal use.(6) Retailers selling such materials to individuals for personal and private use are protected from prosecution for promoting pornography(7) and, additionally, have standing to assert the privacy rights of individuals.(8)

Clearly, developments in Hawaii's law on obscenity have been materially influenced by Hawaii's explicit constitutional right of privacy. Yet, the law has neither escaped nor resolved the two primary dilemmas occasioned by the several First Amendment concerns—including free speech, free press, individual privacy, and personal autonomy—that are necessarily involved in regulating obscene speech. These dilemmas are, first, how to define "obscenity" and, then, having defined the term, identifying the particular acts for which persons can be penalized without thereby censoring and also criminalizing ideas and thoughts protected under the First Amendment. Complicating matters are the facts that Hawaii case law in the area of obscenity remains sparse(9) and that some of the key statutory provisions on obscenity have yet to be interpreted by Hawaii's courts.(10)

Adults and Pornography

Defining Pornography and Community Standards

Hawaii statutes concerned with public health and morals regulate obscenity.(11) Although applicable statutes are collected under a part entitled "Offenses Related to Obscenity,(12) the term "obscenity" is not defined in the statutes themselves. Instead, the statutes prescribe the use of the procedurally oriented *Miller*-based standard(13) to determine that some speech is unprotected and, consequently, regulable under both the First Amendment and the comparable provision in the state constitution(14) because it is deemed to be obscene.(15) The standard, incorporated into Hawaii's statutory definition of pornography,(16) reads:

> Any material . . . is "pornographic" if . . . [t]he average person, applying contemporary community standards(17) would find that, taken as a whole it appeals to the prurient interest[,] [i]t depicts or describes sexual conduct(18) in a patently offensive way[, and t]aken as a whole, it lacks serious literary, artistic, political or scientific merit.(19)

As the definition makes clear, whether material is in fact "obscene" will virtually always require a decision from a jury, which actually determines the definition on a case-by-case basis by following the procedural guidelines of the statute.(20)

"Community standards" providing the operative criteria are determined on a statewide basis.(21) A jury must find that the defendant violated existing community standards.(22) In reviewing a nonjury trial, however, the Hawaii Supreme Court has noted in dicta that patently offensive depiction of deviate sexual activity, such as anal intercourse, has no social or educational value whatsoever.(23) This makes it unclear whether the courts, as a matter of law, may determine that certain acts are patently offensive and that materials depicting them are obscene and therefore not entitled to protection,(24) regardless of statewide community standards. What is certain is that judicial proceedings must be used to determine whether or not material is obscene;(25) police officers cannot declare material to be legally obscene.(26)

The law applies to "materials," a term that is defined to mean any printed matter, visual representation, or sound recording, including "but not limited to books, magazines, motion picture films, pamphlets, newspapers, pictures, photographs, drawings, sculptures, and tape or wire recordings."(27)

The Offense of Promoting Pornography

A person commits the offense of promoting pornography if, for monetary consideration(28) and "knowing of its content and character,"(29) he or she disseminates any material such as "books, magazines, motion picture films, pamphlets, newspapers, pictures, photographs, drawings, sculptures, and tape or wire recordings"(30) which is pornographic.(31) The gravamen of the offense is commercial exploitation.(32)

"'Disseminate' means to manufacture, issue, publish, sell, lend, distribute, transmit, exhibit, or present material or to offer or agree to do the same."(33)

This portion of Hawaii law on obscenity(34) has been held to be not unconstitutionally overbroad or vague.(35) It gives fair warning that a person who distributes hard core pornography is subject to prosecution.(36)

However, the Hawaii Supreme Court has held that the statute is unconstitutional as applied to a person who sells pornographic material to another who acquires it for personal use in the privacy of the individual's home.(37) Under the law, the status and intent of the customer determine the liability of the seller.

The law against "promoting pornography" also applies to production, presentations, or direction of pornographic performances for monetary consideration,(38) and participation "for monetary consideration in that portion of a performance which makes it pornographic."(39) "'Performance' means any play, motion picture film, dance, or other exhibition performed before an audience."(40)

Prior statutory presumptions made it prima facie evidence that a person who promoted pornography "engaged in that conduct with knowledge of the character and content of the material disseminated . . . ."(41) In 1981, the court held this presumption to be unconstitutional.(42) The State has the burden to prove promotion of pornography with the requisite knowledge or awareness beyond a reasonable doubt.(43) Knowledge must be proven, not presumed,(44) although proof may be made by circumstantial evidence.(45)

Promoting pornography is a misdemeanor.(46)

Displaying Indecent Material:Signs, Billboards, Visible Objects

Hawaii law makes it a crime to knowingly or recklessly display indecent matter on "any sign, billboard, or other object visible from any street, highway, or public sidewalk[.]"(47) Prohibited material includes:
a photograph, drawing, sculpture, or similar visual representation of any person of the age of puberty or older:
(a) Which reveals the person with less than a fully opaque covering over his or her genitals, pubic area, or buttocks, or depicting the person in a state of sexual excitement(48) or engaged in an act of sexual conduct or sadomasochistic abuse;(49) and
(b) Which is presented in such a manner as to exploit lust; and
(c) Which lacks serious literary, artistic, political, or scientific value.(50)

It is prima facie evidence that a person who displayed indecent matter "is engaged in that conduct with knowledge of or in reckless disregard of the character, content, or connotation of the material which is displayed."(51) The prosecutor has the burden of proof beyond a reasonable doubt.(52)

Displaying indecent matter is a petty misdemeanor.(53)

Minors and Pornography

Defining Pornography for Minors

Hawaii makes the promotion of pornography to minors(54) a separate offense.(55) Material is pornographic for minors if:

(a) It is primarily devoted to explicit and detailed narrative accounts of sexual excitement, sexual conduct, or sadomasochistic abuse . . . or

. . . .

(b) It contains any photograph, drawing, or similar visual representation of any person of the age of puberty or older revealing such person with less than a fully opaque covering of his or her genitals and public area, or depicting such person in a state of sexual excitement or engaged in acts of sexual conduct or sadomasochistic abuse . . . .(56)

The issue is whether the material "is presented in such a manner that *the average person,* applying contemporary community standards, *would find that,* taken as a whole, *it appeals to a minor's prurient interest;*(57) and . . . [t]aken as a whole, it lacks serious literary, artistic, political or scientific value."(58) The limiting clauses in the definition of "pornographic for minors"(59) are intended to exclude sex education texts, scientific texts, and most works of art and literature when they are not presented in a manner that appeals to the minor's prurient interest or when they possess social value.(60)

The Offense of Promoting Pornography to Minors

Hawaii law prohibiting the promotion of pornography to minors is based on the state's compelling interests represented by its role as parens patriae. (61) In contrast to Hawaii's two misdemeanor offenses relating to promotion of pornography and display of indecent material,(62) promoting pornography to minors is now a class C felony.(63) In 1988, the penalty for promoting pornography to minors was increased from a misdemeanor as an incentive for pornography dealers to inquire as to the age of their customers and to refuse to sell to minors.(64)

A person commits the offense of promoting pornography to minors if:

Knowing its character and content, he disseminates to a minor material which is pornographic for minors; or

Knowing the character and content of a motion picture film or other performance which, in whole or in part, is pornographic for minors, he:

Exhibits such motion picture film or other performance to a minor; or

Sells to a minor an admission ticket or pass to premises where there is exhibited or to be exhibited such motion picture film or other performance; or

Admits a minor to premises where there is exhibited or to be exhibited such motion picture film or other performance.(65)

The offense includes the noncommercial distribution of pornography to minors.(66) A person who lets a minor page through pornographic material on display, the owner of a theatre, a person selling tickets in a ticket booth, and the usher who takes the ticket and admits the minor are subject to the law.(67)

The law banning the promotion of pornography to minors "does not apply to a parent, guardian, or other person in loco parentis to the minor, or to a sibling of the minor, or to a person who commits any act specified therein in his capacity as a member of the staff of any public library."(68)

It "is prima facie evidence that the defendant knew the person to be a minor[]" if the person:

To whom material pornographic for minors as disseminated, or

(a) To whom a performance pornographic for minors was exhibited, or

(b) To whom an admission ticket or pass was sold to premises where there was or was to have been exhibited such performance, or

(c) Who was admitted to premises where there was or was to have been such performance, was at that time, a minor . . . .(69)

The State still has the burden of proof beyond a reasonable doubt, but the statute permits it to present the case to the trier of fact.(70)

Conclusion

Particularly in an intensely multicultural society like Hawaii's, statewide community standards defining "obscenity" may prove difficult if not virtually impossible to articulate. Perhaps Hawaii's sparse case law and the fact that many of its key statutory provisions on obscenity have yet to be interpreted by Hawaii's courts attest to these special challenges inherent in defining "obscenity."

Endnotes

1. Miller v. California, 413 U.S. 15 (1973).
2. Griswold v. Connecticut, 381 U.S. 479, 484 (1965) (noting that penumbras of specific guarantees of the Bill of Rights help give those guarantees life and substance, creating "zones of privacy").
3. Haw. Const. art. I, § 6. The provision reads, in pertinent part: "The right of the people to privacy is recognized and shall not be infringed without a showing of compelling state interest." *Id.*
4. State v. Kam, 69 Haw. 483, 491, 748 P.2d 372, 377 (1988). "[W]e are not bound by United States Supreme Court precedents . . . . [and] are free to give broader privacy protection than that given by the federal constitution." *Id.* (citation omitted).
5. *Id.* at 494, 748 P.2d at 379 ("Reading and viewing pornographic material in the privacy of one's own home in no way affects the general public's rights."); *cf.* Stanley v. Georgia, 394 U.S. 557, 568 (1969) (holding that states may not prohibit private possession in home of pornographic materials), *cited in* State v. Kam, 69 Haw. at 489, 748 P.2d at 376.

6. *Kam*, 69 Haw. at 495, 748 P.2d at 380 ("Since a person has the right to view pornographic items at home, there necessarily follows a correlative right to purchase such materials for this personal use, or the underlying privacy right becomes meaningless."). *Compare* United States v. 12 200-Feet Reels of Super 8 Mm Film, 413 U.S. 123 (1973) (holding that an individual's First Amendment, privacy-based right to possess pornographic material does not give rise to a correlative right to purchase such materials).

7. *Kam*, 69 Haw. at 496, 748 P.2d at 380 (holding that statute prohibiting promotion of pornography cannot be applied to sales to individuals intending such materials for private use and that such application is unconstitutional).

8. *Id.* at 489, 748 P.2d at 376.

9. *See* Jeffrey S. Portnoy, *The Lum Court and the First Amendment*, 14 U. Haw. L. Rev. 395, 405-07 (1992) (reviewing Hawaii Supreme Court decisions during the past 10 years relating to First Amendment issues and noting that the court's willingness to expand federal protections under Hawaii's constitutional provision guaranteeing individuals' right of privacy has been mainly limited to cases involving obscenity).

10. *See, e.g.*, *Kam*, 69 Haw. at 496 n.2, 748 P.2d at 380 n.2 (reserving decision on whether state's compelling interests justify bans on child pornography, "snuff films," depictions of bestiality, obtrusive public displays, showings to captive audiences, sale of pornography to minors, or regulation by zoning of adult businesses).

11. Haw. Rev. Stat. ch. 712 (1993) ("Offenses Against Public Health and Morals").

12. *Id.* pt. II (comprising *id.* §§ 712-1210 to 712-1219.5).

13. Miller v. California, 413 U.S. 15 (1973).

14. Haw. Const. art. I, § 3.

15. 413 U.S. 15, 24; State v. Manzo, 58 Haw. 440, 453-54, 573 P.2d 945, 954 (1977).

16. Haw. Rev. Stat. § 712-1210 cmt. (Supp. 2002).

17. *Id.* § 712-1210.

18. *See id.* §§ 712-1210; 712-1200; 707-700.

19. *Id.* §§ 712-1210.

20. State v. Kam, 68 Haw. 631, 634, 726 P.2d 263, 265 (1986) (holding that court must instruct jury that they must find that community standard exists and has been violated in order to convict of promoting pornography).

21. Haw. Rev. Stat. § 712-1210(1) (Supp. 2002) ("standards of the State"); *see* Trudie Tongg, Recent Development, *Do Community Standards on Pornography Exist?*, 9 U. Haw. L. Rev. 727 (1987).

22. *Kam*, 68 Haw. at 634, 726 P.2d at 265.

23. State v. Han, 63 Haw. 418, 422, 629 P.2d 1130, 1133 (1981) (per curiam) (upholding conviction for promoting pornography after materials sold to an

undercover agent were admitted and viewed as evidence by the trial court).
24. *Cf.* State v. Bumanglag, 63 Haw. 596, 604, 634 P.2d 80, 86 (1981) (noting, in a criminal trial charging defendants with promoting pornography in connection with films seized by the police in violation of First and Fourth Amendment rights, that there are a "'variety of views'" on the United States Supreme Court as to "pertinent distinctions" between "unprotected obscenity from other sexually oriented but constitutionally protected speech").
25. State v. Furuyama, 64 Haw. 109, 116, 637 P.2d 1095, 1100 (1981) (holding police officers' "preconceived seizures" of allegedly obscene materials without first obtaining judicial concurrence unlawful); *see also* State v. Bumanglag, 63 Haw. 596, 606, 634 P.2d 80, 87 (1981).
26. *Bumanglag*, 63 Haw. at 606, 634 P.2d at 87.
27. Haw. Rev. Stat. § 712-1210 (Supp. 2002).
28. *Id.* § 712-1214 cmt., at 312 (noting "Code's limitation to commercial exploitation").
29. *Id.* § 712-1214(1); *see also Bumanglag*, 63 Haw. 596, 617, 634 P.2d 80, 94 (1981) (requiring scienter or awareness).
30. Haw. Rev. Stat. § 712-1210 (Supp. 2002).
31. *Id.* § 712-1214(1)(a).
32. *Bumanglag*, 63 Haw. at 617, 634 P.2d at 93.
33. Haw. Rev. Stat. § 712-1210 (Supp. 2002). It is enough that the defendant sold pornographic material to a plainclothes police officer. State v. Han, 63 Haw. 418, 419-20, 629 P.2d 1130, 1132 (1981).
34. Haw. Rev. Stat. § 712-1214(1)(a) (1993).
35. State v. Kam, 69 Haw. 483, 487-88, 748 P.2d 372, 375 (1988) (quoting State v. Manzo, 58 Haw. 440, 444, 573 P.2d 945, 949 (1977)).
36. *Manzo*, 58 Haw. at 462, 573 P.2d at 958.
37. *Kam*, 69 Haw. at 494, 748 P.2d at 380.
38. Haw. Rev. Stat. § 712-1214(1)(b) (1993).
39. *Id.* § 712-1214(1)(c).
40. *Id.* § 712-1210.
41. *Id.* § 712-1216(1), *held unconstitutional by Bumanglag*, 63. Haw. 596, 634 P.2d 80 (1981).
42. *Bumanglag*, 63 Haw. at 621-22, 634 P.2d at 96-97.
43. Haw. Rev. Stat. § 712-1213 cmt., at 310 (1993).
44. *See Bumanglag*, 63 Haw. at 621, 634 P.2d at 96.
45. *Id.* at 622-23, 634 P.2d at 97.
46. Haw. Rev. Stat. § 712-1214(2) (1993).
47. *Id.* § 712-1211(1). The definition of "place" regulated by the statute is not so broad as to include any public place but is limited to those areas where the public cannot escape confrontation by the display. *Id.* cmt., at 309.
48. "'Sexual excitement' means the condition of the human male or female

genitals when in a state of sexual stimulation or arousal." *Id.* § 712-1210.

49. "'Sadomasochistic abuse' means flagellation or torture by or upon a person as an act of sexual stimulation or gratification." *Id.* § 712-1210.

50. *Id.* §§ 712-1211(1)(a) to 712-1211(1)(c). Subsections (b) and (c) exclude certain works of art from the prohibition. *Id.* § 712-1211 cmt., at 309.

51. *Id.* § 712-1213 (Supp. 1992).

52. *Id.* § 712-1213 cmt., at 310 (1993).

53. *Id.* § 712-1211(2).

54. "'Minor' means any person less than sixteen years old." *Id.* § 712-1210.

55. *Id.* § 712-1215; *see* text accompanying notes 63-72.

56. Haw Rev. Stat. § 712-1210 (Supp. 2002).

57. *Id.* § 712-1210 (emphasis added). Note that an adult viewpoint of "a minor's prurient interest," rather than a "reasonable minor's" viewpoint, forms the basis for the standard; *see infra* note 63 and accompanying text (discussing state's role as parens patriae).

58. *Id.*

59. *Id.*

60. *Id.* § 712-1215 cmt., at 314.

61. *Id.* § 712-1215 cmt., at 314 (1993). Parens patrie refers to the state's function as guardian to persons under legal disability, such as infants. Black's Law Dict. 1003 (6th ed. 1990).

62. *See supra* notes 30-55 and accompanying text.

63. Haw. Rev. Stat. § 712-1215 (1993 & Supp. 2002).

64. *Id.* § 712-1215 cmt., at 315 (citing Haw. Sen. Stand. Comm. Rep. No. 1763, 14th Leg., Reg. Sess. (1988), *reprinted in* 1988 Haw. Senate J. 793; Haw. H.R. Stand. Comm. Rep. No. 1596, 14th Leg., Reg. Sess. (1988), *reprinted in* 1988 Haw. House J. 1394).

65. *Id.* §§ 712-1215(1)(a) to 712-1215(b)(iii).

66. *Id.* cmt., at 314 ("provision not limited to dissemination for monetary gain").

67. *Id.* § 712-1215 cmt., at 314.

68. *Id.* § 712-1215(2); *see also id.* cmt., at 314.

69. *Id.* § 712-1216(2).

70. *Id.* § 712-1216 cmt., at 315.

Chapter 4
Commercial Speech, Advertising, and Public Speech

Commercial speech and advertising are protected under the First Amendment of the United States Constitution and article I, section 4 of the Hawaii Constitution.(1) However, they receive less protection than noncommercial speech(2) and are subject to regulation by federal and state laws.(3)

Hawaii courts, while acknowledging the difficulty of defining "commercial speech," have not articulated a legally precise and comprehensive definition of either the term "commercial speech" or the term "advertising". The lack of such legally unambiguous definitions complicates the issue of whether regulation of commercial activities conflicts with constitutionally based protection of speech occurring in public.

The Hawaii Supreme Court has stated that "[c]ommercial speech includes speech which proposes no more than a commercial transaction"(4) and "[c]ommercial speech is expression related solely to the economic interests of the speaker and its audience."(5) The court has also stated that the cornerstone of commercial speech is the dissemination of information(6) and observed that commercial speech is speech that is not incompatible with the commercial activity of an area in which it occurs.(7)

In Hawaii, government restrictions on commercial speech and advertising are valid if they satisfy a four-part test first set out by the United States Supreme Court in *Central Hudson Gas & Electric Corp. v. Public Service Commission*.(8) First, the commercial speech must concern lawful activity and not be misleading. Regulations on false and misleading speech do not violate free speech rights.(9) Secondly, the asserted government interest must be substantial. If these first two tests are met, the court must then determine whether the regulation directly advances the governmental interest asserted and whether the regulation is narrowly tailored to serve that interest.(10)

Because Hawaii's economy depends to a significant degree on tourism, regulation of advertising in the state has been a highly significant First Amendment issue. The government's traditional interests in protecting consumers from false and misleading advertising is augmented by the need to protect the golden egg of tourism produced by the islands' natural beauty and heavily promoted aloha spirit. Advertising in Hawaii is regulated by both federal and state laws and by county ordinances.(11)

Historical Overview

The pre-statehood case of *Territory v. Scruggs*(12) demonstrated reluctance to protect commercial speech and emphasized that exercise of police powers to ensure public safety does not abridge freedom of press or freedom of speech.(13) *Scruggs* involved a solicitor of subscriptions who challenged a fine and thirty-day jail sentence by unsuccessfully attempting to assert that an ordinance prohibiting canvassing on streets and sidewalks was unconstitutional because it abridged free speech.(14)

The Hawaii Supreme Court held that a state statute enabled the City and County of Honolulu to prohibit "hawking, selling or vending" on its "streets, highways, public thoroughfares, public places, alleys and sidewalks."(15) An ordinance prohibiting a magazine subscription solicitor from using the narrow sidewalks of downtown Honolulu did not, the court stated, abridge free speech or free press.(16) Congestion resulting from such activities provided adequate basis for regulation, notwithstanding First Amendment concerns raised by the defendant.(17)

Then, in the post-statehood case of *State v. Taylor*,(18) the Hawaii Supreme Court effectively upheld a statute prohibiting the placing, leaving, or depositing of goods, wares, or merchandise on public sidewalks.(19) The court, distinguishing the statute from overbroadly defined loitering statutes,(20) cited federal precedent to rule that statutes aimed at limited conduct whose regulation lies within the police power are not invalid merely because they involve First Amendment rights.(22) In the landmark case of *State v. Diamond Motors, Inc.*,(23) the court extended the scope of the police power to validate regulations of commercial speech aimed to preserve aesthetic values.(24)

Then, in its *State v. Bloss* decision,(25) the Hawaii Supreme Court acknowledged that commercial speech is protected speech whose regulation requires judicial scrutiny.(26) The *Bloss* court declared a Honolulu ordinance outlawing the distribution of commercial handbills unconstitutional because it was not the least restrictive means of regulating the commercial speech at issue. The defendant had affixed pockets to the outside of his Volkswagen van to facilitate distribution from a parking stall in Waikiki of handbills about his gun club.(27) Applying the *Central Hudson* test, the court found that while the advertising was neither inaccurate nor misleading, the city's interest in preserving and maintaining the attractiveness of tourism was substantial.(28) The court also acknowledged that there was a direct relationship between the ban on commercial handbilling and the state's interest in preventing nuisances.(29) But, the court invalidated the ordinance, ruling that preserving the attractiveness of tourism in Waikiki could be achieved by regulations less severe than a total ban on commercial handbilling there.(30)

In a case involving the same regulation as subsequently amended, the court again found that the anti-handbilling law, which was intended to preserve the attractiveness of Waikiki, was unconstitutional.(31) "The ordinance totally prohibits protected commercial speech (in an area where such speech would not be incompatible) and provides no alternative channels of communication."(32)

Time, place, and manner restrictions can be used to regulate commercial speech on either public property or in traditional public forums. Although Hawaii courts have never relied on these grounds as a means of upholding commercial speech regulations, they have discussed their applicability to such cases.(33) In *Bloss*, for instance, the court remarked that an ordinance placing a total ban on handbilling in Waikiki was unconstitutional as a time, place, and manner regulation because Waikiki has a high level of commercial activity with which handbilling is not, per se, incompatible.(34) On the other hand, an ordinance prohibiting the sale of merchandise on city streets was held constitutionally valid as a time, place, and manner regulation where it operated to prohibit vendors from selling message-bearing T-shirts on the Waikiki sidewalks.(35)

Yet another ground for restrictions of commercial speech can be found in tort law. It is not a restriction of free speech and press for courts to recognize that an individual has a privacy "right not to have one's name used without his permission as part of an advertising campaign."(36) Thus, tort law principles coupled with privacy rights penumbrally protected by the First Amendment(37) and explicitly guaranteed under the state constitution(38) also provide potential bases for the regulation of advertising.

In a significant recent case asserting unsuccessfully that a publisher of a travel guide should be liable for the injury of a tourist who tried to surf at a beach listed in the travel guide as being safe, the Hawaii Supreme Court declared that a publisher who neither authors nor guarantees the contents of its publication has no duty to warn the public about the accuracy of the contents of its publication.(39) The case, which limits the scope of tort law applicable to commercial speech, acknowledges the potentially chilling effect on free press rights of imposing on publishers absolute liability for the truthfulness of their publications.(40)

Outdoor Signs

To preserve its natural beauty, in part as an economic asset attracting tourism, Hawaii bans outdoor billboards and regulates outdoor signs. In *State v. Diamond Motors, Inc.*,(41) the Hawaii

Supreme Court evaluated the constitutionality of a Honolulu zoning ordinance limiting the height and size of outdoor signs. The court ruled that the ordinance, promulgated to further aesthetic qualities of the state, was a proper exercise of the municipality's police power and did not abridge free speech.(42) The court cited the state constitution, which provides: "The State shall have power to conserve and develop its natural beauty, objects and places of historic or cultural interest, sightliness and physical good order, and for that purpose private property shall be subject to reasonable regulation."(43) Diamond Motors established the principle that beauty alone is a proper community objective attainable through the use of the state's police power.(44)

Hawaii statutes generally prohibit all outdoor advertising visible from a federal or state highway.(45) Exceptions are made for onsite signs advertising the sale or lease of property. Traffic signs and signs identifying scenic or historical attractions are also exempt as are onsite signs advertising business activity. Statutes also prohibit unauthorized signs upon or visible from any highway which imitate, resemble, or interfere with a traffic-control device or which attempt to control traffic.(46) Moreover, the statutes prohibit placing commercial advertising on any traffic sign or signal on any highway.(47) Finally, persons engaged in the outdoor advertising business are subject to state(48) and county regulation.(49)

Advertising by Professionals

Not only outdoor advertising but advertising in any media can be regulated. Advertising regulations in Hawaii are numerous and prove that the public policies for regulation of commercial speech extend beyond aesthetic considerations to regulation of professionals and protection of consumers.

In Hawaii, attorneys must follow a code of professional responsibility,(50) which places certain restrictions on advertising.(51) Hawaii laws regulate advertising by many other types of professionals.

Employment Advertising

Hawaii statutes specifically address discrimination concerns and employment advertising during labor disputes. One statute, which outlaws advertisement containing discriminatory language, is particularly broad. It is unlawful for "any employer or employment agency to print, circulate, or cause to be printed or circulated any statement [or] advertisement . . . which expresses, directly or indirectly, any limitation, specification, or discrimination because of race, sex, age, religion, color, ancestry, physical handicap, marital status, or arrest and court record[.]"(52) However, "bona fide occupational qualifications reasonably necessary to . . . normal operation[s] and which have a substantial relationship to the [position]" are exempt.(53)

Another statute regulates advertisements for employment during a labor dispute. Any advertisement communicated by way of newspapers, posters, letters, radio, or television while a labor dispute "is still in active progress" must disclose the existence of the labor dispute.(54)

Other Advertising Laws and the Regulation of Business Practices

Clearly, Hawaii's advertising laws span the scope of the state's police power to protect the general health, safety, and welfare as well as the community's aesthetic values. Many laws are specifically designed to protect consumers. For example, Hawaii law prohibits the advertising for sale of imitation controlled substances,(55) electronic eavesdropping equipment by unauthorized persons,(56) and drug paraphernalia.(57) The statutes also prohibit commercial advertising by motor vehicle salesmen without revealing the name of their employer when the vehicle is not owned by them,(58) by an unlicensed motor vehicle repair dealer,(59) and by persons whose real estate advertising is discriminatory.(60)

Other Hawaii statutes address unfair competition practices.

For instance, a person may not advertise that the excise tax is not an element of price(61) nor advertise a sale or giveaway at less than cost "with the intent to destroy competition."(62) Similarly, misrepresentations and false advertising by insurance companies as to the benefits, terms, dividends, or surplus paid on their policies are prohibited.(63)

Hawaii's statute on deceptive business practices makes it a misdemeanor when a person engaged in a business, occupation, or profession knowingly or recklessly:

(1) Uses or possesses for use a false weight or measure, or any other device for falsely determining or recording any quality or quantity;

(2) Sells, offers or exposes for sale, or delivers less than the represented quantity of any commodity or service; or

(3) Takes or attempts to take more than the represented quantity of any commodity or service when as buyer he furnishes the weight or measure; or

(4) Sells or offers for sale adulterated(64) commodities; or

(5) Sells or offers or exposes for sale mislabeled(65) commodities.(66)

The section on deceptive business practices was not intended as a comprehensive list of prohibited practices.(67) Rather, statutes outside the Hawaii Penal Code, which specifically address the practice involved, control.(68)

A person engages in deceptive trade practices when he:

(1) Passes off goods or services as those of another;

(2) Causes likelihood of confusion or of misunderstanding as to the source, sponsorship, approval, or certification of goods or services;

(3) Causes likelihood of confusion or of misunderstanding as to affiliation, connection, or association with, or certification by, another;

(4) Uses deceptive representations or designations of geographic origin in connection with goods or services;

(5) Represents that goods or services have sponsorship, approval,

characteristics, ingredients, uses, benefits, or quantities that they do not have or that a person has a sponsorship, approval, status, affiliation, or connection that the person does not have;

(6) Represents that goods are original or new if they are deteriorated, altered, reconditioned, reclaimed, used, or secondhand;

(7) Represents that goods or services are of a particular standard, quality, or grade, or that goods are of a particular style or model, if they are of another;

(8) Disparages the goods, services, or business of another by false or misleading representation of fact;

(9) Advertises goods or services with intent not to sell them as advertised;

(10) Advertises goods or services with intent not to supply reasonably expectable public demand, unless the advertisement discloses a limitation of quantity;

(11) Makes false or misleading statements of fact concerning the reasons for, existence of, or amounts of price reductions; or

(12) Engages in any other conduct which similarly creates a likelihood of confusion or of misunderstanding.(69)

A Hawaii statute defines false or misleading advertising as the knowing or reckless false or misleading(70) statement in any advertisement directed to the public or to a substantial number of persons made in connection with the sale of property or services.(71)

Political Signs and Advertisements

Hawaii's restrictions on outdoor signs and its regulation of advertising have given rise to several cases challenging the constitutionality of restrictions placed on political signs. In all of these cases, decided by Hawaii's federal court, ordinances restricting the use of outdoor political signs have been declared unconstitutional for not being content-neutral and for not being the least restrictive means of regulating political advertising. The cases also illustrate that political speech enjoys greater protection than commercial speech.

In *Ross v. Goshi*,(72) the federal district court held that political campaign signs are a form of expression protected by the First Amendment.(73)

In *Aiona v. Pai*,(74) a case originating in Hawaii, the Ninth Circuit summarily ruled that a state statute banning movable political campaign signs from sidewalks and areas next to highways was unconstitutional.(75) In so holding, the Ninth Circuit effectively upheld a key method of political campaigning used by nearly every candidate running for election (or reelection) in the state. Candidates and their supporters, holding and waving campaign signs, turn out in force along major arteries during peak commuting hours.

Most recently, in *Runyon v. Fasi*,(76) the federal district court held that preserving aesthetic values in Honolulu was not a sufficiently compelling reason to uphold a statute banning political signs in residential neighborhoods. The federal district court explained that the statute was not content-neutral and that less drastic means were available for accomplishing its intended objective.(77)

State statutes require that political advertisements give the name and address of the candidate, committee, party, or person paying for the ad.(78) If the ad is paid for by someone other than the candidate or his committee, it must "contain a notice in a prominent location that the literature or advertisement is published, broadcast, televised, or circulated with the approval and authority of the candidate."(79) If a person does so without the approval and authority of the candidate, the advertisement must contain a notice to that effect.(80)

"Advertisement" includes any communication which supports or opposes the nomination or election of a candidate(81) or identifies, supports, or opposes an issue or question which may appear on the next election ballot.(82)

Private Regulation of Speech in Public

Also conceptually related to regulation of commercial speech are issues relating to private regulation of speech in public. Dispositive to the outcome of such cases in Hawaii has been the private status of the entities attempting to regulate free speech activities on private property they controlled.

In the case of *Estes v. Kapiolani Women's and Children's Medical Center,*(83) the Hawaii Supreme Court emphasized that private policies against on-premise solicitation do not abridge free speech if the premises do not constitute a public forum and the policies as enforced allow speakers alternate channels of communication.(84) *Estes* involved the removal of anti-abortion activists from entry walkways of a private hospital. In a tersely reasoned decision(85) focusing primarily on the limits of the state action doctrine,(86) the court held that the hospital was not a traditional public forum and implied that alternate channels of communication remained open to the protestors who were attempting to distribute literature and make their views known to hospital patrons, staff, and visitors.(87)

Two cases involving political leafletting have subsequently further delineated the application of the state action doctrine in Hawaii. In *Zimmerman v. Nakatani,*(88) the plaintiff, Robert Lee Zimmerman, a dark-horse candidate for the United States Senate, successfully challenged the right of a private organization that had been endorsed and subsidized by the state, the Hawaii State Farm Fair, to prevent him from leafletting near the entrance to the fairgrounds. The fair is held annually on public school grounds made available to the private organization at no cost.(89) On the basis of several factors by which the fair held itself out as a state-endorsed and co-sponsored function open to the public—including the fact that a government official from the state department of agriculture also sat on the fair's board, which had promulgated the fair's no-solicitation policy—the court found state action making the fair's no-solicitation regulation unconstitutional as enforced.(90) The following year, the fair allowed groups to distribute information at the fair if they rented a booth, an imposition of time, place, and manner restrictions on fairground solicitations held by the United States Supreme Court to be constitutional in *Heffron v. International Society for Krishna Consciousness*.(91)

In *Zimmerman v. Northwestern Mutual Life Insurance Co.*,(92) Zimmerman, protesting his exclusion from the State Farm Fair, was again prevented from leafletting, this time in Tamarind Park, an extensively used but privately owned park in the heart of Honolulu's downtown financial district.(93) In this case, the federal district court found that the park's regulations and their enforcement against Zimmerman did not constitute state action, that the park was not a public forum, and that adequate alternative channels of communication were available to Zimmerman.(94)

Endnotes

1. State v. Bloss, 64 Haw. 148, 637 P.2d 1117 (1982) (holding regulations against handbilling in Waikiki—as applied to owner of gun club—unconstitutionally vague and not the least restrictive means of serving a protected governmental interest), *cert. denied*, 459 U.S. 824.
2. *Id.* at 157, 637 P.2d at 1123-24 (discussing development of federal case law protecting commercial speech).
3. Virginia Pharmacy Bd. v. Virginia Consumer Council, 425 U.S. 748 (1976).
4. *Bloss*, 64 Haw. at 153, 637 P.2d at 1123 (citing *Virginia Pharmacy Bd.*, 425 U.S. at 762).
5. *Id.* (quoting Central Hudson Gas v. Public Serv. Comm'n, 447 U.S. 557, 561 (1980)).
6. *Id.* at 154, 637 P.2d at 1123.
7. State v. Hawkins, 64 Haw. 499, 501, 643 P.2d 1058, 1060 (1982) (regulating handbilling in Waikiki held unconstitutional).
8. 447 U.S. 557 (1980).
9. *In re* Corey, 892 F.2d 829 (9th Cir. 1989) (upholding Hawaii district court's injunction against false claims regarding land).
10. State v Bloss, 64 Haw. 148, 158, 637 P.2d 1117, 1125 (1982) (quoting *Central Hudson*, 447 U.S. at 566).
11. *See e.g.*, Haw. Rev. Stat. § 445-113 (1993) (state law authorizing regulation of outdoor signs by counties).

12. 43 Haw. 71 (1958).

13. *Id.* at 74.

14. *Id.* at 72.

15. *Id.* at 73 (citing Rev. L. of Haw. § 149-86(2) (1955) (enabling city "[t]o regulate and control for any and every purpose" the areas enumerated)).

16. *Id.* at 74.

17. *Id.* at 75.

18. 49 Haw. 624, 425 P.2d 1014 (1967).

19. *Id.* at 633, 425 P.2d at 1019-20.

20. *See* State v. Bloss, 62 Haw. 147, 613 P.2d 354 (1980) (separate case from earlier cited *Bloss* case; holding loitering statue unconstitutionally vague).

21. *Taylor*, 49 Haw. at 633, 425 P.2d at 1020 (citing Adderley v. Florida, 385 U.S. 39 (1966)). *See also Bloss*, 64 Haw. 147, 152-53, 613 P.2d 354, 358 (1980) (challenging successfully loitering statute held to be unconstitutionally vague).

22. 49 Haw. at 633, 425 P.2d at 1020.

23. 50 Haw. 33, 429 P.2d 825 (1967) (upholding Hawaii regulations categorically prohibiting billboards, here in an industrial district).

24. *See infra* notes 40-43 and accompanying text.

25. 64 Haw. 148, 637 P.2d 1117, *cert. denied*, 459 U.S. 824 (1981).

26. *Id.* at 154-55, 637 P.2d at 1123 (calling protection of commercial speech "a recent development of constitutional jurisprudence").

27. *Id.* at 150, 637 P.2d at 1120.

28. *Id.* at 158-59, 637 P.2d at 1125-26.

29. *Id.* at 162, 637 P.2d at 1128.

30. *Id.*

31. State v. Hawkins, 64 Haw. 499, 501, 643 P.2d 1058, 1059 (1982).

32. *Id.* at 501, 643 P.2d at 1059-60.

33. *See, e.g.*, State v. Bloss, 64 Haw. at 161, 637 P.2d at 1127.

34. *Id.* at 160-61, 637 P.2d at 1127.

35. One World One Family v. City & County of Honolulu, 76 F.3d 1009 (9th Cir. 1996).

36. Fergerstrom v. Hawaiian Ocean View Estates, 50 Haw. 374, 377, 441 P.2d 141, 144 (1968) (holding that homeowners' privacy was invaded by misappropriation of their names and likeness in advertising brochures issued by a real estate developer).

37. Griswold v. Connecticut, 381 U.S. 479, 484 (1965).

38. Haw. Const. art. I, § 6.

39. Birmingham v. Fodor's Travel Publ'ns, Inc., 75 Haw. 359, 833 P.2d 70 (1992).

40. *Id.* at 368, 833 P.2d at 75-76. The court refused to impose liability under theories of misrepresentation, strict product liability, or breach of implied

warranty. *Id.* at 366-75, 833 P.2d at 75-78.
41. 50 Haw. 33, 429 P.2d 825 (1967).
42. *Id.* at 36, 429 P.2d at 827.
43. Haw. Const. art. IX, § 7.
44. 50 Haw. at 36, 429 P.2d at 827.
45. Haw. Rev. Stat. § 264-72 (1993).
46. *Id.* § 291C-36(a).
47. *Id.* § 291C-36(b).
48. *Id.* § 445-112.
49. *Id.* § 445-113.
50. *See, e.g.*, Oahu Plumbing & Sheet Metal, Ltd. v. Kona Constr., 60 Haw. 372, 590 P.2d 570 (1993).
51. Haw. Code of Prof. Respon. 7.2.
52. Haw. Rev. Stat. § 378-2(3) (1993).
53. *Id.* § 378-3(2).
54. *Id.* § 379-3.
55. *Id.* § 329C-2(d).
56. *Id.* § 803-43.
57. *Id.* § 329-43.5(d).
58. *Id.* § 437-4.
59. *Id.* § 437B-11.5.
60. *Id.* § 515-3(6).
61. *Id.* § 237-49.
62. *Id.* § 481-3.
63. *Id.* § 431:13-103(a)(1).
64. "'Adulterated' means varying from the standard of composition or quality" set by statutory prescription, administrative regulation, or commercially established usage. *Id.* § 708-870(2).
65. "'Mislabeled' means varying from the standard of truth or disclosure in labeling" set by statutory prescription, administrative regulation, or established commercial usage or represented as another's product. *Id.* §§ 708-870(3)(a), (b).
66. *Id.* § 708-870.
67. *Id.* § 708-870 cmt.
68. *Id.* § 708-870(5).
69. *Id.* §§ 481A-3(a)(1) to -3(a)(12). Common law actions or actions brought under other statutes are not affected by this section. *Id.* § 481A-3(c).
70. A "misleading statement" includes an offer to sell property or to provide services without intention to sell or provide the product or service at the offered price or lower, without intention to sell it in sufficient quantity to meet public demand, unless quantity is advertised, or without intention to sell it at all. *Id.* §§ 708-871(2)(a) to -871(2)(c).

71. *Id.* § 708-871(1).
72. 351 F. Supp. 949 (D. Haw. 1972).
73. *Id.* at 953.
74. 516 F.2d 892 (9th Cir. 1975).
75. *Id.* at 892-93.
76. 762 F. Supp. 280 (D. Haw. 1991).
77. *Id.* at 284-85 (comparing regulation to ones struck down in Metromedia, Inc. v. City of San Diego, 452 U.S. 490 (1991)).
78. Haw. Rev. Stat. § 11-215(a) (1993).
79. *Id.* § 11-215(b)(1).
80. *Id.* § 11-215(b)(2).
81. *Id.* § 11-191(1)(A).
82. *Id.* § 11-191(1)(B).
83. 71 Haw. 190, 787 P.2d 2216 (1990).
84. *See id.* at 196, 787 P.2d at 220.
85. *See* Lisa A. Laun & Mark D. Lofstrom, Estes v. Kapiolani Women's and Children's Medical Center: *State Action and the Balance Between Free Speech and Private Property Rights in Hawaii*, 13 U. Haw. L. Rev. 233 (1991) (analyzing the court's opinion as being too narrowly focused on state action to the detriment of applicable First Amendment analysis but concurring that correct result was reached).
86. The doctrine is usually invoked when recovery is sought from the government and concerns the issue of what involvement, typically indirect, by the state serves to make an injurious act, typically by a private person, that of the state. *See* Black's Law Dict. 1407 (6th ed. 1991).
87. *Id.* at 197, 787 P.2d at 221.
88. Civ. No. 88-00488 ACK (D. Haw. 1988).
89. Order Affirming Judgment, No. 90-16158 (9th Cir., filed Feb. 10, 1992), *aff'g* Civ. No. 88-00488 ACK (D. Haw. 1988).
90. Order Granting in Part and Denying in Part Plaintiffs' and Defendants' Motions for Summary Judgment (filed Dec. 27, 1988), Civ. No. 88-00488 ACK (D. Haw. 1988).
91. 452 U.S. 460 (1981).
92. Civ. No. 89-00484 (D. Haw. 1989).
93. Order Granting Defendant's Motion for Partial Summary Judgment (filed Oct. 23, 1990), Civ. No. 89-00484 ACK (D. Haw. 1989).
94. *Id.* at 3-4.

Chapter 5

Hawaii's Sunshine Law (Access to Places)

The Hawaii Open Meetings Law (also known as the state's "Sunshine Law") is based on the premise that "in a democracy, the people are vested with the ultimate decision-making power. Governmental agencies exist to aid the people in the formation and conduct of public policy."(1) The Hawaii Sunshine Law protects the people's "right to know" by requiring government entities to conduct their business "as openly as possible."(2)

In cases involving open meetings laws, the plaintiffs assert that a government agency's decision, which will directly or indirectly affect them, should be set aside because the agency violated the Sunshine Law.(3) Alternatively, the media may challenge meetings of public officials to which they and the public are not invited by public notice or to which they and the public are not provided access.(4) Generally, Sunshine Law cases in Hawaii to date have dealt with either or both of two threshold issues: whether the body holding the meeting is in fact a government "board" governed by the state's Sunshine Law,(5) and/or whether the body's convening is in fact a "meeting" requiring public notice.(6)

Open Meetings

The provisions of the law requiring open meetings(7) are to be liberally construed,(8) and provisions permitting exceptions(9) are strictly construed against closed meetings.(10) Generally, the Hawaii Sunshine Law mandates that "every meeting of all boards shall be open to the public and all persons shall be permitted to attend any meeting . . . submit data, views, or arguments, in writing . . . or to present oral testimony on any agenda item."(11)

A "board" is defined as "any agency, board, commission, authority, or committee of the State or its political subdivisions which is created by constitution, statute, rule, or executive order, to have supervision, control, jurisdiction or advisory power over specific matters and which is required to conduct meetings and to take official actions."(12) The law does not apply, however, to advisory bodies without decision-making power derived from statutes,(13) thus creating a potential loophole that is likely to remain the subject of controversy.(14)

State and county governments are covered by the law.(15) However, the law does not apply to the judicial branch;(16) quasi-judicial boards exercising adjudicatory functions(17) unless excepted;(18) and legislative bodies governed by their own rules and procedures.(19) Also exempted are certain executive meetings,(20) advisory committees,(21) and fact-finding hearings.(22)

Non-governmental bodies are not governed by the Sunshine Law. When the University of Hawaii student newspaper sought access to meetings of other student organizations, the Attorney General advised the University Regents and Administrators that the "ASUH (Associated Students of the University of Hawaii) and other student organizations did not fall within the definition [of 'board' in the law] and thus are not subject to the requirements imposed by the State Sunshine Law."(23)

Public Notice Requirement

The Hawaii Sunshine Law requires public notice of any regular, special, or rescheduled meeting and of executive meetings anticipated in advance.(24) The notice must include an agenda of the items to be considered and the date, time, and place of the meeting.(25) Boards must maintain a list of and mail notices to persons requesting notification of meetings.(26)

An unresolved issue involves whether a reconvened meeting requires separate notice to the public. In 1992, the University of Hawaii Board of Regents while reviewing candidates for the position of President of the University, adjourned a meeting to a later date. When the media demanded notice of and access to the reconvened meeting, the Board of Regents refused and requested an opinion on the matter. The Attorney General opined that the reconvened meeting did not require separate notice.(27) However, the Attorney General's position was arguably at odds with even the office's own prior opinion.(28) Responding, at least in part, to the pressure of a potential lawsuit, the Board of Regents decided to provide separate notice of the reconvened meeting, notwithstanding the Attorney General's advice, and surprised many in the media by divulging the names of the finalists being considered for the position.

A board is required to file its notice in the office of the lieutenant governor or the appropriate county clerk's office at least six working days before the meeting.(29) Trustees of the Office of Hawaiian Affairs (OHA) were recently confronted with the importance of correctly computing the period required for advance notice. The Attorney General sided with members of the public who objected to the notice provided by OHA of a forthcoming meeting and opined that both the day of notice and fractions of days are excluded from the six-day advance notice requirement.(30) Because OHA had incorrectly calculated the period of required advance notice, its notice was ineffective under the statute.

Notice must be posted at the meeting site whenever feasible.(31)

The agenda as posted must list specific "items" or "matters"; general headings are insufficient to comply with the law's notice provisions.(32) A board can change its agenda once filed only by a two-thirds recorded vote of all members,(33) but it cannot add items of "reasonably major importance . . . [which] affect a significant number of persons."(34) Furthermore, if it is not convened in a scheduled meeting, a board can consider items of reasonably major importance "only at a meeting continued to a reasonable day and time."(35)

Meetings

Emergency Meetings

Emergency meetings are permitted "if [two-thirds of the members of] a board find[] that an imminent peril to the public health, safety, or welfare requires a meeting in less time than is ... [required for the filing of a notice]."(36) The law requires that a board:

provide, in writing, reasons for the emergency meeting;

(a) file the emergency agenda and findings with the appropriate office;

(b) contact persons who requested notification as soon as practicable by mail or telephone; and

(c) limits its action to those which must be taken on or before the date on which a properly noticed meeting would have been held.(37)

Executive Sessions

Hawaii law permits executive sessions closed to the public upon an affirmative vote of two-thirds of the members present at an open meeting.(38) To be valid, the affirmative vote must constitute a majority of all board members including those not present and those not yet appointed, i.e., to vacancies.(39) The board must publicly announce its reason for the closed meeting and record and enter the vote of each member into the minutes of the open meeting.(40)

Meetings may be closed to the public only for purposes specified under the exceptions(41) to the open meeting requirement.(42) Generally, a board may not decide or deliberate toward a decision unless the purpose of the closed meeting is to:

(1) consider personal information relating to the application of licenses and the hire, evaluation, dismissal, or discipline of officers or employees where privacy is a concern, unless the affected individual requests an open meeting;

(2) deliberate upon negotiations relating to labor and land

acquisition;

(3) consult with the board's attorney regarding its powers, duties, privileges, immunities, and liabilities;

(4) investigate criminal misconduct;

(5) consider sensitive matters related to public safety or security;

(6) to consider matters relating to the solicitation and acceptance of private donations; or

(7) to deliberate or make a decision on a matter concerning information that must be kept confidential under state or federal law or court order.(43)

Interactions Among Members

Two or more members of an agency may communicate or interact privately between themselves for certain purposes.(44) The Sunshine Law does not cover these communications or interactions.(45) The purposes for which these communications or interactions may be undertaken include gathering information about official agency matters as long as no commitment to vote is made or sought;(46) investigating a matter relating to the official business of the agency;(47) presenting, discussing, or negotiating any position which the agency has adopted at a meeting of the agency;(48) and discussing the selection of the agency's officers.(49)

Administrative Meetings

An agency cannot adopt, amend, or repeal any rule without first holding a public hearing.(50) The law requires that the adopting agency give at least twenty days notice by publication in a newspaper of general circulation.(51) The notice must include the substance of the proposed rule and the date, time, and place of the public hearing where the public may testify.(52) Notices must be mailed to persons who requested notification in advance.(53)

An agency must "[a]fford all interested persons [the] opportunity to submit data, views, or arguments, orally or in writing . . . [and must] fully consider all written and oral submissions respecting the proposed rule."(54) Upon adoption of the new, repealed, or changed rule and at the request of and interested person, the adopting agency must issue a statement of the principal reasons for its decision.(55)

The adoption, amendment, or repeal of a state or county rule is subject to the approval of the governor or mayor.(56) The governor or mayor can waive the open meeting and notice requirement if a state or county agency is required to promulgate rules as a condition of receiving federal funds.(57) The agency must publish the substance of the rule change in a newspaper of general circulation prior to the waiver.(58)

If an agency finds that an emergency exists, it may adopt a rule for a maximum period of 120 days.(59) An emergency exists where there is "an imminent peril to the public health, safety, or morals or to livestock and poultry health. . . ."(60) The agency must state in writing its reasons for finding that an emergency exists, but it may proceed without prior notice or hearing.(61) Minutes of meetings of boards are public records(62) and must be available to the public within thirty days of the meeting.(63)

Violating the Act

If the open meeting(64) and notice(65) requirements of the Hawaii Sunshine Law are violated, any final action taken by the offending government body is voidable upon proof of a wilful violation.(66) Any person may bring suit to require compliance, prevent violations, or to determine whether a public body falls within the scope of the law.(67) The court may order payment of attorneys' fees and costs to the prevailing party.(68) A suit alleging a wilful violation of the Hawaii Sunshine Law must be brought within ninety days of the final action.(69) "Any person who wilfully violates any provisions of . . . [the open meetings law is] guilty of a misdemeanor, and upon conviction, may be summarily removed from the board unless otherwise provided by law."(70)

An agency may enforce its decision while a suit is under

review.(71) However, a reviewing court may order a stay if: the party bringing the suit is likely to prevail, irreparable damage will result in the absence of a stay, no irreparable damage will result from a stay order, *and* a stay order is in the public interest.(72)

Media Access to News Sites

The media's need for access to areas where news is occurring often raises issues that are, if not exactly concurrent with, then at least related to issues addressed by the Sunshine Law. A case arising in the late 1970s demonstrated how media access can be curtailed by law enforcement efforts. Police arrested reporters covering activists demonstrating on a runway of Hilo Airport in violation of the airport's administrative regulations.(73) Although the trial court dismissed criminal charges lodged against the reporters because it invalidated the regulations under which the reporters had been arrested, it refused, except under limited circumstances not pertaining to the case, to grant the media any greater rights of access to disaster and crime scenes than the general public possesses.(74)

Media Access to Prisons

When journalists attempt to interview prisoners, they frequently encounter prison regulations and limitations imposed by the correctional system itself. Prisoners' First Amendment rights are weighed against the penological interest of the prison system in arriving at determinations whether such regulations are constitutional from the perspective of the prisoner.

In the Hawaii case of *Mujahid v. Sumner*,(75) the federal district court declared that prison regulations prohibiting prisoners from corresponding with journalists absent "a bona fide friendship... established prior to commitment"(76) were unconstitutional.(77) The court noted that in addition to requiring that prison regulations impinging on prisoners' free speech must show

> a rational connection between the regulation and the asserted penological interest, the court also considers whether there are alternative means of exercising the right that remain open to prison inmates, the impact of accommodation of the asserted constitutional right will have on guards and other inmates and on the allocation of prison resources generally, and the absence of ready alternatives as evidence of the reasonableness of the regulation.(78)

Although important in establishing that prisoners have a right to communicate with the media, the *Mujahid* decision does not address nor guarantee the media a right to communicate with prisoners. Regulations allow prison officials to deny the media access to the prisons and specifically to deny the media access to individually identified prisoners.

Endnotes

1. Haw. Rev. Stat. § 92-1 (1993).
2. *Id.*
3. *See, e.g.*, Chang v. Planning Comm'n of County of Maui, 64 Haw. 431, 643 P.2d 55, (1982) (contesting zoning and planning decision); Outdoor Circle v. Harold K.L. Castle Trust, 4 Haw. App. 633, 675 P.2d 784 (1983) (holding agency decision voidable only upon showing of wilful violation of Sunshine Law).
4. *See, e.g.*, KHON-TV v. Ariyoshi, Civ. No. 78696 (Haw. 1st Cir. Ct. Aug. 1983) (challenging unsuccessfully meetings of Governor's Ad Hoc Group on Water); Applicability of the Haw. Sunshine Law to the Comms. of the [Univ. of Haw.] Bd. of Regents, Att'y Gen. Op. 85-27 (Nov. 27, 1985) (challenging successfully failure to provide notice of committee meetings held without the quorum needed to conduct official business).
5. KHON-TV, Civ. No. 78696 (holding that ad hoc group was not a government board because it had no decision making power and was comprised of volunteers; appeal to state supreme court dismissed as

moot); *see also* Applicability of State Sunshine Law to Dep't of Agric.'s Advisory Comm. on Plants and Animals and Subcomms., Att'y Gen. Op. 90-7 (Sept. 12, 1990) (allowing consulting experts denominated as "subcommittees" of a government advisory board to operate outside the state's Sunshine Law requirements).

6. Applicability of the Haw. Sunshine Law to the Comms. of the [Univ. of Haw.] Bd. of Regents, Att'y Gen. Op. 85-27 (Nov. 27, 1985) (requiring notice even if board is short of quorum in meeting to discuss official business); Maui Corp. Counsel Op. (Oct. 17, 1980) (stating that adjournment sine die [without delay] terminates the meeting and invokes the requirement that notice be given of the meeting's resumption). *But see* Att'y Gen. Ltr. (1992) (opining that notice of reconvened meeting of university's governing board is not required).

7. Haw. Rev. Stat. § 92-3 (1993).

8. *Id.* § 92-1(2).

9. *Id.* §§ 92-4, 92-5.

10. *Id.* § 92-1(3).

11. *Id.* § 92-3.

12. *Id.* § 92-2(1).

13. KHON v. Ariyoshi, Civ. No. 78696 (Haw. 1st Cir. Ct. filed July 27, 1983) (holding that voluntary ad hoc committee was without power to render decisions; case subsequently dismissed on appeal to state supreme court as being moot because the committee's meetings had concluded).

14. *Id.*; *see also* Applicability of State Sunshine Law to Dep't of Agric.'s Advisory Comm. on Plants and Animals and Subcomms., Att'y Gen. Op. 90-7 (Sept. 12, 1990) (exempting technical consultants from Sunshine Law meetings requirements).

15. Haw. Rev. Stat. § 92-2(1) (1993).

16. *Id.* § 92-6(a)(1).

17. Quasi-judicial boards include, but are not limited to, the Hawaii Labor Relations Board, Labor and Industrial Relations Appeals Board, Hawaii Paroling Authority, Civil Service Commission, Board of Trustees, Employees' Retirement System of the State of Hawaii, Criminal Injuries Compensation Commission, and State Ethics Commission. *Id.* § 92-6(a)(2).

18. *Id.* § 92-6(b) (excluding Land Use Commission from exception for adjudicatory bodies).

19. *Id.* § 92-10; *see also* Judgment and Order, Abercrombie v. Senate, S.P. No. 6126 (Haw. 1st Cir. Ct. May 23, 1984) (denying plaintiffs' request for access to legislative budget committee records governed by legislative bodies' rules), *appeal dismissed,* 67 Haw. 671 (1984); Grade v. Kunimura, Civ. No. 66451 (Haw. 1st Cir. Ct. July 13, 1981) (holding that state House and Senate rules requiring open meetings were consistent with article III, section 12 of the Hawaii Constitution).

20. Att'y Gen. Ltr. (Oct. 17, 1985) (determining that governor's cabinet is not an agency; therefore, its meetings are not covered by the Hawaii Sunshine Law).

21. Att'y Gen. Ltr. (Feb. 25, 1986) (concluding that State Civil Defense Advisory Council is not a "board" because meetings, quorum requirements, and official action are not required).

22. Op. Honolulu Corp. Counsel M83-65 (1983) (holding that the transcript of a fact-finding hearing conducted by the Office of Human Resources is not a public record).

23. Att'y Gen. Op. No. 85-18, at 2 (Sept. 6, 1985).

24. Haw. Rev. Stat. § 92-7(a) (1993).

25. *Id.* § 92-7(a).

26. *Id.* § 92-7(e).

27. Att'y Gen. Ltr. (1992) (unavailable for public release) (opining, reportedly, that notice of reconvened meeting of University's Board of Regents is not required; apparently repudiating unspecified prior opinion letter).

28. *See* Applicability of the Haw. Sunshine Law to the Comms. of the [Univ. of Haw.] Bd. of Regents, Att'y Gen. Op. 85-27 (Nov. 27, 1985) (requiring notice even if board is short of quorum in meeting to discuss official business); *see also* Maui Corp. Counsel Op. (Oct. 17, 1980) (stating that adjournment sine die [without delay] terminates meeting leading to requirement that notice be given of resumption).

29. Haw. Rev. Stat. § 92-7(b) (1993).

30. Computation of Time Pursuant to HRS section 92-7, Att'y Gen. Op. No. 92-06 (Aug. 20, 1992) (interpreting the statutory requirement to exclude the day of giving notice and refusing to recognize fractions of days).

31. Haw. Rev. Stat. § 92-7(b) (1993).

32. Agenda and Minutes of Haw. State Comm'n on the Status of Women, Att'y Gen. Op. 85-2, at 3 (Feb. 4, 1985).

33. Haw. Rev. Stat. § 92-7(d) (Supp. 2002).

34. *Id.*

35. *Id.*

36. *Id.* § 92-8. The wording does not specify six days, perhaps allowing agencies a reasonable accommodation for administrative processing of meeting notices if the meeting will occur in, e.g., six to eight days.

37. *Id.*

38. *Id.* § 92-4.

39. *Id.*

40. *Id.*

41. *Id.* § 92-5.

42. *Id.* § 92-4.

43. *Id.* § 92-5(a).

44. *Id.* § 92-2.5.

45. *Id.* § 92-2.5(f).

46. *Id.* § 92-2.5(a).

47. *Id.* § 92-2.5(b)(1).

48. *Id.* § 92-2.5(b)(2).

49. *Id.* § 92-2.5(c).

50. *Id.* § 91-3(a)(1).

51. *Id.*

52. *Id.*

53. *Id.*

54. *Id.* § 91-3(a)(2); *see also id.* § 92-3.

55. *Id.* § 91-3(a)(2).

56. *Id.* § 91-3(c).

57. *Id.* § 91-3(d).

58. *Id.*

59. *Id.* § 91-3(b).

60. *Id.*

61. *Id.*

62. *Id.* § 92-9(b); *see also* Att'y Gen. Op. 64-4 (1964) (holding that agency hearing transcript is public record).

63. Haw. Rev. Stat. § 92-9(b) (1993).

64. *Id.* § 92-3.

65. *Id.* § 92-7.

66. *Id.* § 92-11.

67. *Id.* § 92-12(c).
68. *Id.* § 92-12(c).
69. *Id.*
70. *Id.* § 92-13.
71. *Id.* § 92-12(d).
72. *Id.* (emphasis added).
73. State v. Fredo, Crim. No. 5710 et. seq. (Haw. 3d Cir. 1979).
74. Decision and Order on Motion to Dismiss, at 37-39, State v. Fredo, Crim. No. 5710 (Haw. 3d Cir. Mar. 5, 1979) (citing, inter alia, Branzburg v. Hayes, 408 U.S. 665, 684-85 (1972)).
75. Civ. No. 92-00060 (D. Haw. 1992).
76. Haw. Admin. R. 17-203-11(g)(4) and (i).
77. Order Granting Summary Judgment in Favor of Plaintiff Declaring Hawaii Administrative Rules 17-203-11(g)(4) and (i) Unconstitutional (Now. 12, 1992) at 6-13, *Mujahid v. Sumner*, Civ. No. 92-00060 (D. Haw. 1992).
78. *Id.* at 11-12.

Chapter 6
Access to Records: Hawaii's Open Records Law

Hawaii's Open Records Law, the Uniform Information Practices Act (Modified) (UIPA), which seeks to protect the public interest by "[o]pening up . . . government processes to public scrutiny and participation,"(1) replaced earlier statutory provisions governing access to government records.(2) The fundamental mandate of the new law is that, unless "restricted or closed by law," "all government records are open to public inspection."(3) The media has the same rights of access to government records as the public. (4)

Illustrative of the type of case commonly involved in disputes between the media and government agencies over access to government records was a pre-UIPA case involving Department of Health records concerning Honolulu sewage treatment facilities.(5) After a weekly newspaper had published a story reporting on EPA violations at a new sewage treatment plant, Department of Health officials refused further access to the records. The *Honolulu Advertiser* successfully sued for access to the records. In his order requiring that the newspaper be given access to the records, the judge cited the constitution, statutes, properly evoked regulations, or court rules as providing possible grounds for an exemption from the public inspection requirement applicable to government records.(6) As none of these exemptions applied, the *Advertiser* was given access to the department's records, which revealed little of significant interest. The case, however, demonstrated the value of freedom of information statutes to counteract a tendency of government to restrict access to records generated in the process of executing and fulfilling government functions.

Hawaii adopted the UIPA following extensive testimony and public discussion coordinated by a governor-appointed committee on public records and privacy.(7) The provisions of the prior open records laws that were the subject of major criticisms were those that restricted access to governmental records if the records contained any "confidential" information that could identify any individual thereby invading his or her privacy.(8) The effect of this provision was to deny access to many public records. Testimony at the hearings on the proposed changes in the state's open records law called for a balancing test weighing the public's interest in access against the individual's interests in confidentiality in order to determine rights of access.(9) The committee favored and the legislature passed a law providing "maximum public access to records with a narrow range of exceptions,"(10) a law that effectively operates on a "presumption of openness."(11) The Governor's Committee on Public Records and Privacy noted several reasons for adopting a law that would employ a balancing test based on a presumption of access:

(1) Government is only a custodian of records belonging to the people;

(2) Lack of access leads to distrust of government;

(3) Lack of access leads to ignorance of government and its activities;

(4) Public access should follow use of public funds;

(5) Records advancing the rule of law should be open;

(6) Additional manpower costs and frustration of public employees required by access is outweighed by increased accountability and responsiveness of government;

(7) Classifying records as "personal" and "private" should not be synonymous as there are a number of "personal" items of information about which there should be no expectation of privacy;

(8) Rights of free speech and free press necessarily include a right to know; and

(9) Those who choose to act in the public arena must bear public scrutiny.(12)

The Legislature acknowledged the public testimony received during hearings(13) and declared that, given the legislatively endorsed view "that an open government is the cornerstone of our democracy,"(14) "the current confusion and conflict which surround the existing records laws [was] plainly unacceptable."(15) Accordingly, the legislature adopted the UIPA in order to "clarify the law relating to government records;"(16) it "wipe[d] the slate clean and adopted a new law"(17) that "addresses the often competing public and privacy interests in a single new law which categorizes various types of requestors while establishing certain countervailing individual privacy interests."(18)

Under the UIPA, any individual or legal person—"corporation, government, or governmental subdivision or agency, business trust, estate, trust, partnership, association, or any other legal entity"(19)—may request access to government records.(20) The public's interest in having government be conducted "as openly as possible" is necessarily "tempered by a recognition of the [constitutional](21) right [of individuals] to privacy."(22) The UIPA (as modified and adopted in Hawaii) serves five purposes:

(1) to promote disclosure,(23)

(2) to provide accurate, relevant, timely, and complete government records,(24)

(3) to enhance governmental accountability through a policy of access,(25)

(4) to enhance governmental accountability to individuals when it collects, uses, and disseminates information relating to them,(26) and

(5) to balance individuals' privacy interests and the public's interest in access.(27)

Generally, government records are open to the public unless allowing access to the documents would constitute a "clearly unwarranted invasion of personal privacy";(28) frustrate "a legitimate government function";(29) or violate a state or federal statute or a state or federal court order.(30) A fourth exception to the UIPA's broad disclosure requirements protects government records relating to "prosecution or defense of any judicial or quasi-judicial action to which the State or any county is *or may be* a party."(31)

Burnham Broadcasting Co. v. County of Hawaii,(32) the first Hawaii court case to interpret the new law as it pertains to the media, ended in summary judgment for the media plaintiffs.(33) The media, in order to report on a sensational Christmas Eve rape/murder, after repeated refusals of their requests, sued the police and fire departments to obtain transcripts and copies of tapes of calls made to the 911 emergency assistance number.

The County attempted to argue that disclosure was not required because it would interfere with apprehension of criminal suspects and because disclosure would interfere with privacy interests of the victim's family. The victim's family waived their privacy interests, although the media plaintiffs did not concede that the privacy rights of a deceased's family could justify nondisclosure of government records. In reply to the County's argument that nondisclosure served the public's interest in apprehending the suspects, the plaintiffs asserted that nondisclosure for this reason did not fall within the narrow exceptions to the UIPA's broad mandate of disclosure of government records.(34) The County attempted to argue that its nondisclosure prevented prejudicial publicity to which a still-to-be-apprehended suspect might be subjected, thereby protecting Sixth Amendment rights.(35) The County also argued that the government had a right not to disclose the information under its prosecutorial privilege and that disclosure would interfere with the legitimate government function of law enforcement.(36) Plaintiffs pointed out that nondisclosure tied to the UIPA's law enforcement exception only pertained to materials that would not be discoverable in civil litigation and that the

County could not prove frustration of a legitimate government function merely upon the say-so of police officers.(37)

The court agreed with the media plaintiffs and held that all telephone and radio communications concerning the incident were public records to which the media were entitled to have access.(38) It also awarded the plaintiffs all of their attorneys' fees and costs, effectively forcing the county to pay for its agencies' intransigence.(39)

Government Agencies Covered by the UIPA

The UIPA applies to all government agencies at both the state and county levels, including the executive, legislative, and judicial branches of government. The Act broadly defines an "agency" as:

> any unit of government in this State, any county, or any combination of counties; department; institution; board commission; district; council; bureau; office; governing authority; other instrumentality of state or county government; or corporation or other establishment owned, operated, or managed by or on behalf of this state or any county . . . .(40)

The Office of Information Practices (OIP), a division within the Attorney General's Office, has the responsibility to interpret the law and make rulings at the behest of governmental agencies or individuals seeking disclosure.(41) The definition has been interpreted to protect from disclosure records of certain activities of recognized "agencies," i.e., nonadministrative records of the judiciary(42) including lists of judicial nominees submitted to the governor.(43) The UIPA does apply, however, to the administrative records of the judiciary(44) including, e.g., obtaining certified abstracts of motor vehicle operating records.(45)

Public Access

All government records are open to the public unless access is restricted by law.(46) Agencies must make unrestricted government records available for inspection and copying during regular business hours.(47) Each agency must ensure that the public has reasonable access to copying facilities.(48)
An agency is not required to prepare a record summary unless the information is readily retrievable by the agency in the form requested.(49) In addition, each agency may adopt rules to protect records from theft, loss, defacement, alteration, or deterioration and to prevent excessive interference with the performance of other statutory duties.(50)
Government records available for public inspection and duplication under the UIPA include:

(1) agency rules of procedure and statements of general policy;(51)
(2) final opinions and orders made in the adjudication of cases;(52)
(3) government purchasing information including bid results;(53)
(4) gubernatorial pardons, commutations, and information concerning an individual's presence at a correctional facility;(54)
(5) land ownership, transfer, and lien records;(55)
(6) results of environmental tests;(56)
(7) minutes of meetings required by law to be public;(57)
(8) name, address, and occupation of any person borrowing funds from a state or county loan program, and the amount, purpose, and status of the loan;(58)
(9) payroll records of public works contracts;(59)
(10) contract hires employed by agencies;(60)
(11) building permit information;(61)
(12) rosters of license and permit holders;(62)
(13) limited personnel information;(63)
(14) information collected for the purpose of being made available to the public;(64) and

(15) information in or compiled from transcripts or minutes of public meetings.(65)

Exceptions to the General Rule of Public Access

Invasion of Privacy

The UIPA does not require the disclosure of government records whose disclosure would constitute a "clearly unwarranted invasion of personal privacy".(66) The law accommodates the constitutional guarantee of "informational privacy" as it concerns "the possible abuses in the use of highly personal and intimate information in the hands of government or private parties"(67) while simultaneously allowing the government to compile and disseminate data.(68) Particularly in the case of personal records, the UIPA invasion-of-privacy exception is concerned with constitutional protection accorded "personal autonomy privacy".(69)

A two-step test is used to determine whether disclosure of records would cause an invasion of personal privacy: (1) whether the privacy interest is "significant";(70) and, (2) if the privacy interest is "significant", whether the public interest in disclosure outweighs the privacy interest of the individual.(71) If the privacy interest is not "significant", a "scintilla" of public interest will preclude a finding of unwarranted invasion of privacy.(72)

The UIPA is intended to protect from public disclosure an individual's "significant" privacy interest in information:(73)

(1) Relating to an individual's medical, psychiatric, or psychological history, diagnosis, condition, treatment, or evaluation;

(2) Identifiable as part of a criminal investigation, except as needed to prosecute or continue investigating the crime;

(3) Relating to an individual's eligibility for social services or welfare benefits;

(4) Contained in an agency's personnel files;(74)

(5) Relating to an individual's nongovernment employment history;

(6) Describing an individual's finances, income, assets, liabilities, net worth, bank balances, financial history or activities, or credit worthiness;(75)

(7) Regarding an inquiry into an individual's fitness to obtain or hold a license, except records of a proceeding resulting in the discipline of a licensee, the current place of employment and required insurance coverage of licensee, and record of complaints against licensee and disposition thereof; and

(8) Regarding a personal recommendation or evaluation.

A trial court has enjoined public disclosure by the University of Hawaii's president of the names of university faculty union members who were charged with sexual harassment by student complaints filed with the school's Equal Opportunity Officer, notwithstanding the OIP's determination that the complaints constitute a formal charges that are publicly disclosable under chapter 92F.(76)

The court decided the motion for injunction on the basis of provisions in the union's contract, which required that information about "the settlement of greivances and the imposition of workplace discipline [on] employees covered by the [union's] agreement" be kept confidential.(77) Granting the union standing to bring its motion for an injunction against the University President's announced intention to publicly release the names of faculty members facing sexual harrassment charges, the court noted that the union had "demonstrated [that the public release by] the University of its member's name [would] cause the member to suffer irreparable injury."(78) The court held that "[t]he balance of harm, the likelihood of success on the merits, and the public interest weigh in favor of granting [the union it's motion for] a preliminary injunction" against public release of its member's names.(79)

While it enjoined the University's president from releasing

any names of union members charged with sexual harrassment, the court nevertheless refused on First Amendment grounds to enjoin the University's student-run newspaper from publishing the names. The court's action demonstrates that even when the First Amendment prevents imposition of restrictions on the press, the court may use indirect restraints, i.e., court-imposed restraints on the sources of information, as a means of attempting to limit public disclosure of allegedly highly personal information. Subsequently, the University's student-run newspaper published two of the names.

During its 1993 session, Hawaii's Legislature passed a law approved by the Governor that amended the UIPA to include within the listing of records "in which an individual has a substantial privacy interest"(80):

The following information related to employment misconduct that results in an employee's suspension or discharge:

(a.)   The name of the employee;
(b.)   The nature of the employment related misconduct;
(c.)   The agency's summary of the allegations of misconduct;
(d.)   Findings of fact and conclusions of law; and
(e.)   The disciplinary action taken by the agency;
        when the following has occurred:
   (1) the highest non-judicial greivance adjustment procedure timely invoked by the employee or the employee's representative has concluded;
   (2) a written decision sustaining the suspension or discharge has been issued after this procedure; and
   (3) thirty calendar days have elapsed following the issuance of the decision;
        provided that this subparagraph shall not apply to a county police department officer with respect to misconduct that occurs while the officer is not acting in the capacity of a police officer.(81)

The amended law secures from public disclosure information about public employees' misconduct "while formal grievance procedures are still in progress" but refuses "to provide further protection from disclosure of misconduct when the employee has exhausted nonjudicial grievance procedures, and has been suspended or discharged."(82)

In contrast to information about private individuals, the public has an interest in disclosure of "official information that sheds light on an agency's performance of its statutory purpose"(83) and in information which sheds light upon the conduct of government officials.(84) Thus, in a case involving predecessor provisions of Hawaii's UIPA,(85) the Hawaii Supreme Court upheld a constitutionally mandated county ethics code requirement(86) that "regulatory employees" disclose their income and financial interests to the County Board of Ethics.(87) In *Nakano v. Matayoshi*, the court noted "that the expectation of financial privacy of public `officials having significant discretionary or physical powers' is not protected to the same extent as that of other citizens."(88)

More recently, the case of *State v. Klattenhoff*(89) demonstrated that even a private citizen's expectation of privacy regarding his personal financial information can be overridden by public interests. The *Klattenhoff* court held that a subpoena of personal bank records in criminal proceedings does not violate either state or federal privacy rights because such records are business records owned by banks.(90) Accordingly, it noted, an individual has no protectable expectation of privacy in such records.(91)

Examples of information whose disclosure constitutes a "clearly unwarranted invasion of personal privacy" under the UIPA are:

(1) pension benefits of retired public employees;(92)
(2) birthdate and social security number;(93)
(3) home telephone number;(94) and
(4) lists and scores of unsuccessful applicants for government positions.(95)
(5) the fact and status of a person's application to a university graduate program.(96)

(6) individuals' identities in city ethics commission opinions.(97)

In accordance with the constitutional basis for the invasion-of-privacy exception to public disclosure of government records under the UIPA, protection is generally limited to "highly personal and intimate information."(98)
Examples of information where the public interest in disclosure *outweighs* the individual's privacy interest are:
(1) the identity, training, and experience of *successful applicants and nominees* for government positions;(99)
(2) the name, island-wide rank, area code, application date, and deferral status of individuals on the Department of Hawaiian Home Lands waiting list;(100)
(3) the non-medical vacation and sick leave records of government employees;(101)
(4) the names of firearms owners and descriptions of handguns registered with the Honolulu Police Department;(102) and
(5) the identity of public employees charged with sexual harassment, the status of proceedings following filing of such complaint, and agency disciplinary proceedings.(103)

The protective privilege against disclosure of records which constitute an invasion of privacy applies only to natural persons.(104) It is personal: death extinguishes it.(105) Finally, it is waivable.(106)

Frustration of Legitimate Government Function

The UIPA does not require disclosure of government records that must be kept confidential in order to avoid the "frustration of a legitimate government function".(107) Records which may be protected from disclosure include:
(1) Records or information compiled for law enforcement purposes;
(2) Materials used to administer an examination which, if disclosed, would compromise the validity, fairness, or

objectivity of the examination;

(3) Information which, if disclosed, would raise the cost of government procurements or give a manifestly unfair advantage to any person proposing to enter into a contract or agreement with an agency, including information pertaining to collective bargaining;

(4) Information identifying or pertaining to real property under consideration for future public acquisition, unless otherwise available under State law;

(5) Administrative or technical information, including software, operating protocols, and employee manuals, which, if disclosed, would jeopardize the security of a record-keeping system;

(6) Proprietary information, such as research methods, records and data, computer programs, and software, and other types of information manufactured or marketed by persons under exclusive legal right, owned by an agency, or entrusted to it;

(7) Trade secrets or confidential commercial and financial information;

(8) Library, archival, or museum material contributed by private persons to the extent of any lawful limitation imposed by the contributor; and

(9) Information that is expressly made nondisclosable or confidential under federal or state law or protected by judicial rule.(108)

Examples of records that have been protected because disclosure would frustrate a legitimate government function include:

(1) Terms of settlement agreements between the State and certain defendants when the State continues to be involved in ongoing litigation with other defendants in the same case;(109)

(2) Drafts and notes of agency employees that are "predecisional" and "deliberative" in nature;(110)

(3) University of Hawaii self-study and program review reports;(111) and

(4) Videotaped confessions.(112)

(5) Identity of informant complaining of alleged violation of laws.(113)

(6) Identity of persons under investigation for a crime but who have not been arrested or publicly charged with a crime.(114)

Examples of records not protected under the legitimate government function exception include:

(1) Names of persons serving on the University of Hawaii School of Law's Admissions Committee;(115)

(2) ABA accreditation reviews of the University of Hawaii Law School;(116)

(3) Airport concessionaire revenue audit reports;(117)

(4) Certain management training course materials of the Department of Personnel Services;(118)

(5) Unit prices in lump sum public contract bids;(119)

(6) Honolulu Police Department's Standards of Conduct;(120) and

(7) Information contained in police blotters or arrest logs.(121)

The government successfully invoked the UIPA's "frustration of legitimate government function" exception in a case ultimately reviewed by the Hawaii State Supreme Court and involving the state's open meetings and open records laws.(122) The plaintiff, by virtue of his Hawaiian ancestry, claimed an indirect interest in profits receivable from the development of a prime site in downtown Honolulu.(123) After a state-chartered development corporation set up by the legislature to develop the site had held public meetings and tentatively selected a developer for the site, the plaintiff filed a suit seeking, among other things, disclosure of all bid proposals submitted to the development corporation. The court upheld the circuit court's grant of a motion for summary judgment in favor of the defendant development corporation. The summary judgment allowed the development corporation to refuse to disclose to the plaintiff the bids received and the tentatively accepted development proposal's contents pending finalization of a long-term lease on the site.(124)

Following(125) the reasoning of the OIP,(126) the state supreme court noted that the confidentiality exception would remain operative "until the [development corporation] completed its selection procedure and made a final choice of a developer for the complex."(127) The court reasoned that under the UIPA(128), the bid development proposals "are government records that, by their nature, must be kept confidential in order to avoid the frustration of a legitimate government function...." (129)

The basic concern underlying the frustration-of-governmental-function exception to the UIPA's disclosure requirements is enhancement of the quality of government decision-making processes by shielding deliberative processes from public scrutiny that might chill intra-agency candor and consideration of policy options.(130) This provision is similar to one found in the Freedom of Information Act (FOIA)(131) and was not found in the UIPA's predecessor statutes.

Records Closed by Statute or Court Order

The UIPA does not require the disclosure of government records which are protected from disclosure by state or federal statute or by order of a state or federal court.(132) Records closed by law include tax returns,(133) child abuse reports,(134) vital statistics records,(135) and records of the Department of Social Services and Housing.(136)

Other Exceptions

The UIPA does not require the disclosure of drafts, budget worksheets, and unfiled reports of legislative committees nor disclosure of the personal files of legislators.(137)

In the pre-UIPA case of *Abercrombie v. Senate*,(138) a state senator (now a U.S. Congressman) and five colleagues joined the excutive director of Common Cause, a citizens' lobbying group, to challenge the denial of their request for copies of the seven-volume state budget worksheets used by the state's Senate committees. The budget worksheets outline the line-by-line expenses comprising each appropriation debated in the legislative committees, while the legislative bills only outline the amounts sought to be appropriated. The worksheets, restricted to conference rooms and closely guarded during committee recesses and at other times when they are not in use by committee members, typically contain notes on the general negotiability of and on each legislator's negotiations affecting any budget item. When the final budget is published, this commentary documenting the negotiations is omitted.(1394)

The circuit court determined that the state budget worksheets used in legislative committees were "merely internal, preliminary work papers prepared by the conferees or their staff to assist the conferees, and to be used only in their discussions and negotiations during the conference sessions" and that "[t]he rules of the Senate provide that the Clerk of the Senate shall `have charge of all records of the Senate,'" which did not include the disputed documents.(140) On appeal, the State Supreme Court dismissed the case on the grounds that the controversy was moot. Although the case was decided under the public records provisions of the state's Sunshine Law,(141) which were subsequently repealed upon enactment of the UIPA,(142) the circuit court's ruling would most likely have been the same under section 92F-13(5) of the UIPA, which specifically protects from disclosure documents that are material to the deliberative processes of the legislature.(143)

Also excepted from UIPA disclosure requirements are government records pertaining to the prosecution or defense of any judicial action in which the State or any county may be a party, to the extent that such records would not be discoverable.(144) The exception encompasses agency records of preliminary investigations.(145) In the case of records concerning judicial enforcement proceedings, a two-step test is used once it is determined that the disputed records would not be discoverable: (1) whether a proceeding is pending or imminent, and (2) whether release of information might reasonably be expected to cause articulable harm.(146)

There is no exception in the UIPA for requests that an agency regards as too burdensome.(147)

Interagency Disclosure

An agency may not disclose records to other agencies unless disclosure is:

(1) necessary for the performance of the requesting agency's duties and functions and is (a) compatible with the purpose for which the information was collected; and (b) consistent with the reasonable expectations of use under which the information was provided;

(2) to the State archives;

(3) to another agency, another state, or the federal government, or foreign law enforcement agency or authority, if the disclosure is (a) for the purpose of law enforcement authority authorized by law; and (b) pursuant to a written agreement or written request or a verbal request made under exigent circumstances;

(4) to state, federal, or foreign criminal law enforcement agency if the information is limited to an individual's name and other identifying particulars, including present and past places of employment;

(5) to a foreign government pursuant to an executive agreement, compact, treaty, or statute;

(6) to the legislature or committees thereof;

(7) pursuant to court order;

(8) to agents or officials of another agency, another state, or the federal government for the purpose of auditing or monitoring a program receiving federal, state, or county funding;

(9) to the State Legislative Reference Bureau, legislative auditor, or the ombudsman;

(10) to the department of human resources development, county personnel agencies, or line agency personnel offices for the performance of their respective duties and functions, including employee recruitment and examination, classification and compensation reviews, the administration and auditing of

personnel transactions, the administration of training and safety, workers compensation, and employee benefits and assistance programs, and for labor relations purposes; or
(11) otherwise subject to disclosure under the UIPA.(148)

Records otherwise confidential under the UIPA's privacy and frustration-of-government-function exceptions may be subject to interagency disclosure.(149) Agencies are not required to disclose otherwise confidential information to other agencies, but may do so under the criteria set forth in *Hawaii Revised Statutes* section 92F-19. Hawaii does not restrict inter-agency disclosures to the same extent as does the federal FOIA.(150) Interagency disclosure does not waive protection against public disclosure when records are otherwise protectable.(151)

Individual Access to Personal Records
The UIPA sets forth separate criteria governing the access by individuals to their own "personal records." A "personal record" may be any item, collection, or grouping of information about an individual that is maintained by an agency.(152) The law requires that an agency which maintains any accessible personal records shall make that record available to the individual to whom the record pertains.(153) Disclosure of the record by the agency must be reasonably prompt and in a reasonably understandable form.(154)

There are five exceptions and limitations to an individual's access to personal records. An agency is not required to grant an individual access to personal records:
(1) maintained by an agency that performs any activity pertaining to crime prevention, including "criminal history record information," e.g., information compiled at any stage of the enforcement of criminal laws;
(2) revealing the identity of a confidential source;
(3) consisting of testing material used solely to determine employment or licensing qualifications, the disclosure of

which would compromise the objectivity or fairness of testing;
(4) including investigative reports relating to judicial or administrative proceedings against the individual; or
(5) required to be withheld from the individual by statute or order.(155)

Appealing Denials of Access

Denials of Access In General

Anyone denied access to government records may bring an action in court against the withholding agency at any time within two years of the agency's refusal to disclose.(156) Unlike the federal Freedom of Information Act,(157) the UIPA does not condition judicial review of an agency's refusal to disclose on exhaustion of administrative remedies.(158) The agency has the burden of justifying its denial.(159)

In the alternative, a person may appeal to the Office of Information Practices without prejudicing their right to pursue matters in judicial proceedings.(160) If the OIP determines that a record should be disclosed, the withholding agency shall comply with the decision.(161)

Denials of Access to and Agency Refusal to Correct Personal Records

An individual entitled to access to personal records has the right to have any factual errors corrected by the agency maintaining the record.(162) Anyone denied the opportunity to correct a personal record may appeal to the state circuit courts(163) or to the Office of Information Practices.(164)

However, individuals seeking access or corrections to personal records about them maintained by an agency must first exhaust agency procedures relating to such requests.(165) The basic procedures require that the individual make a request and allow the agency ten days to respond to a request to review a personal record(166) (extendable to twenty days upon written notice from the agency within the initial ten-day period)(167), twenty days to respond to a written request for corrections to a personal record,(168) and thirty days after the agency provides notice of its denial as a final determination regarding a refusal to correct a personal record.(169)

When denying a request for a correction to a personal record, the agency must "[i]nform the individual in writing of its refusal . . ., the reason for its refusal, and the agency procedures for review of the refusal."(170) When the agency makes a final determination that it will not correct a personal record, it must (1) "[p]ermit . . . the individual to file in the record a concise statement" recording his objection to the agency's refusal(171) and (2) inform the individual of procedures to obtain judicial relief.(172)

Liability and Attorney Fees

Criminal Liability for Disclosure or Release of Confidential Government Records

Intentional disclosure or release of government records or information "explicitly described by confidentiality statutes" "with actual knowledge that disclosure is prohibited" can render an agency officer or employee(173) or a person gaining access by means of "false pretense, bribery, or theft"(174) liable for criminal prosecution.(175) Intentional disclosure or release is a misdemeanor, unless otherwise provided by statute.(176)

Good faith participation in disclosure or nondisclosure of government records, however, will render the individual government employee or participant immune to civil and criminal liability.(177) The immunity does not extend to governmnet entities.(178)

Agency Liability for Failure to Grant Access or Correct Personal Records

An agency knowingly or intentionally violating the UIPA's provisions on personal records may be liable for no less than $1000 in actual damages if it refuses to properly maintain records.(179) Conversely, if an individual brings a frivolous claim seeking access against an agency maintaining a disputed personal record, the court may assess reasonable attorneys' fees and costs against the complainant.(180)

The agency may also be assessed reasonable attorneys' fees and costs if the "complainant has substantially prevailed"(181) in securing access to agency records. In the *Burnham Broadcasting Co. v. County of Hawaii* case, in which the media plaintiffs prevailed on a motion for summary judgment, the state circuit court pursuant to section 92F-15(d) awarded the plaintiffs their attorneys' fees and costs.(182) As a general rule, courts have been inclined to award attorney's fees against government agencies that have been found to improperly deny access to records.

Endnotes

1. Haw. Rev. Stat. § 92F-2 (1993).
2. *Id.* ch. 92, pt. 5, comprising *id.* §§ 92-50 to 92-52 ("Public Records;" repealed 1988), and ch. 92E ("Fair Information Practice (Confidentiality of Personal Record)," comprising *id.* §§ 92E-1 through 92E15) (enacted 1980, repealed 1988).
3. *Id.* § 92F-11.
4. Houchins v. KQED, Inc., 438 U.S. 1, 16 (1978). In *Donrey Media Group v. Ikeda*, 959 F. Supp. 1280 (D. Haw. 1996), the federal district court held that the Hawaii County Clerk's office violated the Equal Protection Clause of the Fourteenth Amendment when it denied members of the media access to voter registration affidavits for purposes of news coverage, but allowed access to the affidavits to other persons for other reasons. The court reasoned that the media could not be singled out for denial of access because its right of access is no different from that of the public.
5. Advertiser v. Yuen, S.P. No. 4997 (Haw. 1st Cir. 1979).
6. Order Allowing Inspection of State of Hawaii Department of Health Records at 2, Advertiser v. Yuen, S.P. No. 4997 (Haw. 1st Cir. Oct. 19, 1979).

7. *See* Report of the Governor's Committee on Public Records and Privacy (1987) (four-volume report containing analysis and testimony).

8. Haw. Rev. Stat. ch. 92E (1985) (repealed 1988).

9. 1 Report of the Governor's Committee on Public Records and Privacy 67 (1987).

10. *Id.*

11. *Id.*

12. *Id.* 67-68.

13. Haw. H.R. Stand. Comm. Rep. No. 342, 14th Leg., Reg. Sess. (1988), *reprinted* in Haw. House J. 969, 969-70 (1988).

14. Haw. H.R. Conf. Comm. Rep. No. 112, 14th Leg., Reg. Sess. (1988), *reprinted in* 1988 Haw. House J. 817, 817.

15. *Id.*; Haw. Sen. Conf. Comm. Rep. No. 235, 14th Leg., Reg. Sess. (1988), *reprinted in* 1988 Haw. Senate J. 689, 689.

16. Haw. Sen. Conf. Comm. Rep. No. 235, 14th Leg., Reg. Sess. (1988), *reprinted in* 1988 Haw. Senate J. 689, 689; Haw. Stand. Comm. Rep. No. 342, 14th Leg., Reg. Sess. (1988), *reprinted in* 1988 Haw. House J. 969, 969-70

17. Government Op. Comm., Stand. Comm. Rep. No. 2580, 14th Leg., Reg. Sess. (1988), *reprinted in* 1988 Haw. Senate J. 1093, 1093.

18. Haw. H.R. Fin. Comm., Stand. Comm. Rep. No. 726, 14th Leg., Reg. Sess. (1988), *reprinted in* 1988 Haw. House J. 1101.

19. Haw. Rev. Stat. § 92F-3 (1993) (definitions).

20. *See id.* § 92F-11(b).

21. Haw. Const. art. I, §§ 6, 7.

22. Haw. Rev. Stat. § 92F-2 (1993).

23. *Id.* § 92F-2(1).

24. *Id.* § 92F-2(2).

25. *Id.* § 92F-2(3).

26. *Id.* § 92F-2(4).

27. *Id.* § 92F-2(5).

28. *Id.* § 92F-13(1).

29. *Id.* § 92F-13(3).

30. *Id.* § 92F-13(4).

31. *Id.* § 92F-13(2) (emphasis added).

32. Civ. No. 92-61 (Haw. 3d Cir. Ct. filed Feb. 14, 1992).

33. Order Granting Plaintiffs' Motion for Summary Judgment, Burnham Broad. Co. v. County of Haw., Civ. No. 92-61 (Haw. 3d Cir. Ct. entered Mar. 27, 1992).

34. Memorandum in Support of Plaintiffs' Motion for Summary Judgment, Burnham Broad. Co. v. County of Haw., Civ. No. 92-61 (Haw. 3d Cir. Ct. filed Mar. 6, 1992).

35. Defendant County of Hawaii's Memorandum in Response to Plaintiffs'

Motion for Summary Judgment, Burnham Broad. Co. v. County of Haw., Civ. No. 92-61 (Haw. 3d Cir. Ct. filed Mar. 10, 1992).

36. *Id.*

37. Plaintiff's Reply to Defendant County of Hawaii's Memorandum in Response to Plaintiff's Motion for Summary Judgment, Burnham Broad. Co. v. County of Haw., Civ. No. 92-61 (Haw. 3d Cir. Ct. filed Mar. 19, 1992).

38. *Id.*

39. Order Granting Plaintiffs' Motion for Attorneys' Fees and Costs, Burnham Broad. Co. v. County of Haw., Civ. No. 92-061 (Haw. 3d Cir. Ct. granted May 13, 1992).

40. Haw. Rev. Stat. § 92F-3 (1993).

41. Established pursuant to Haw. Rev. Stat. § 92F-41, the OIP's primary functions are to provide advisory opinions to the public and to government agencies regarding implementation of the UIPA and to serve as an appeals agency to mediate disputes over access to government records. Haw. Rev. Stat. § 92F-41 (1993 & Supp. 2002). On February 26, 1999, following public hearings, the OIP's administrative rules, "Agency Procedures and Fees for Processing Government Records Requests," took effect. These rules may be may be found in Chapter 71, Title 2, of the Hawaii Administrative Rules.

42. *See id.* § 92F-3.

43. Judicial Selection Comm'n's List of Nominees to Fill Judicial Vacancy, OIP Op. Ltr. 92-3 (Mar. 19, 1992).

44. Jeffrey S. Portnoy & Mark D. Lofstrom, Tapping Officials' Secrets: The Door to Open Government in Hawaii (Reporters Comm. for Freedom of the Press, 2d ed. 1992).

45. Public Access to Certified Abstracts of Motor Vehicles Operating Records, OIP Op. Ltr. No. 90-4 (Jan. 29, 1990).

46. Haw. Rev. Stat. § 92F-11(a) (1993).

47. *Id.* § 92F-11(b); Order Granting Plaintiffs' Motion for Summary Judgment, Burnham Broad. Co. v. County of Haw., Civ. No. 92-0161 (Haw. 3d Cir. Ct. entered Mar. 27, 1992) (citing statutory provision specifically).

48. Haw. Rev. Stat. § 92F-11(d) (Supp. 1992); Order Granting Plaintiffs' Motion for Summary Judgment, Burnham Broad. Co. v. County of Haw., Civ. No. 92-0161 (Haw. 3d Cir. Ct. entered Mar. 27, 1992) (citing statutory provision specifically).

49. Haw. Rev. Stat. § 92F-11(c) (Supp. 1992).

50. *Id.* § 92F-11(e).

51. *Id.* § 92F-12(a)(1).

52. *Id.* § 92F-12(a)(2).

53. *Id.* § 92F-12(a)(3); *see also* Purchase of Service Proposal Rating Sheets, OIP Op. Ltr. No. 91-14 (Aug. 28, 1991) (requiring disclosure of identity of government employees evaluating requests for purchase of services).

54. Haw. Rev. Stat. § 92F-12(a)(4) (1993).

55. *Id.* § 92F-12(a)(5); *see also* DOT Statewide Airport Property Appraisals, OIP Op. Ltr. No. 91-10 (July 18, 1991) (refusing to protect from disclosure Department of Transportation airport property appraisals).

56. Haw. Rev. Stat. § 92F-12(a)(6) (1993).

57. *Id.* § 92F-12(a)(7).

58. *Id.* § 92F-12(a)(8).

59. *Id.* § 92F-12(a)(9).

60. *Id.* § 92F-12(a)(10).

61. *Id.* § 92F-12(a)(11).

62. *Id.* § 92F-12(a)(13).

63. *Id.* § 92F-12(a)(14).

64. *Id.* § 92F-12(a)(15).

65. *Id.* § 92F-12(a)(16).

66. *Id.* § 92F-13(1).

67. Stand. Comm. Rep. No. 69, *reprinted in* 1 Proceedings of the Const. Convention of Haw. of 1978, at 674 (1980) (explaining intent of privacy provision adopted as Haw. Const. art. I, § 6).

68. *Id.*

69. Stand. Comm. Rep. No. 69, *reprinted in* 1 Proceedings of the Const. Convention of Haw. of 1978, at 674 (1980).

[T]he right of privacy [protected by Haw. Const. art. I, § 6] encompasses the common law right . . . of tort privacy. This [right] recogni[zes] that the dissemination of private and personal matters . . . can cause mental pain and distress far greater than bodily injury. . . . [T]his right of privacy includes the right of an individual to tell the world to "mind your own business". . . . [and] gives each and every individual the right to control certain highly personal and intimate affairs of his own life.

Id. See also Jon M. Van Dyke et al., *The Protection of Individual Rights Under Hawai`i's Constitution*, 14 U. Haw. L. Rev. 309 (1992).

70. Haw. H.R. Conf. Comm. Rep. No. 112-88, 14th Leg., Reg. Sess. (1988), *reprinted in* 1988 Haw. House J. 817, 818; Haw. Sen. Conf. Comm. Rep. No. 235, 14th Leg., Reg. Sess. (1988), *reprinted in* 1988 Haw. Senate J. 689, 690.

71. Haw. Rev. Stat. § 92F-14(a) (Supp. 1992).

72. Haw. H.R. Conf. Comm. Rep. No. 112-88, 14th Leg., Reg. Sess. (1988), *reprinted in* 1988 Haw. House J. 817, 818; Haw. Sen. Conf. Comm. Rep. No. 235, 14th Leg., Reg. Sess. (1988), *reprinted in* 1988 Haw. Senate J. 689, 690.

73. Haw. Rev. Stat. § 92F-14(b) (Supp. 1992).

74. *See* Inter-Agency Disclosure of Health Fund Membership Lists, OIP Op. Ltr. No. 91-18 (Oct. 15, 1991) (protecting agency personnel data).

75. Applications for Appointment to Bds. and Comm'ns, OIP Op. Ltr. No. 91-8 (June 24, 1991) (protecting information about applicant's financial status).

76. Disclosure of Sexual Harassment Complaint and Disciplinary Action Taken Against Univ. of Haw. Faculty Member, OIP Op. Ltr. No. 90-12 (Feb. 26, 1990).

77. Order Granting Plaintiff's Motion for Preliminary Injunction 1-2, UHPA v. University of Haw., Civ. No. 91-0035-01 (Haw. 1st Cir. filed Feb. 7, 1991) (Milks, J.).

78. *Id.* at 2.

79. *Id.*

80. Haw. Rev. Stat. § 92F-14 (1993 & Supp. 2002).

81. Act 191, 17th Leg., Reg. Sess. (1993) (enacting Haw. Sen. 1363 to amend Haw. Rev. Stat. § 92F-14).

82. Haw. Sen. Conf. Rep. No. 61, 17th Leg., Reg. Sess. (1993).

83. Disclosure of an Individual's Birthdate and Social Security Number, OIP Op. Ltr. No. 90-7, at 7 (Feb. 9, 1990) (quoting United States Dep't of Justice v. Reporters Comm. for Freedom of the Press, 109 S.Ct. 1468, 1481 (1989)).

84. Disclosure of Information Relating to the Vacation and Sick Leave of Agency Officers and Employees, OIP Op. Ltr. No. 90-17, at 7 (Apr. 24, 1990) (citing federal case); *see also* Disclosure of Sexual Harrassment Complaint and Disciplinary Action Taken Against Univ. of Haw. Faculty Member, OIP Op. Ltr. No. 90-12 (Feb. 26, 1990).

85. Haw. Rev. Stat. § 92E-1 (1985).

86. Hawaii County Code § 2-91.1.

87. Nakano v. Matayoshi, 68 Haw. 140, 706 P.2d 814 (1985).

88. Jeffrey S. Portnoy, *The Lum Court and the First Amendment*, 14 Univ. Haw. L. Rev. 395, 416 (1992) (quoting *Nakano*, 68 Haw. at 149, 706 P.2d at 819, in discussion of privacy jurisprudence in Hawaii).

89. 71 Haw. 598, 801 P.2d 548 (1990).

90. *Id.* at 606, 801 P.2d at 552 (citing U.S. v. Miller, 425 U.S. 435, 440-43 (1976)).

91. *Id.*

92. Disclosure of Information re the Pension Benefits of Retired Pub. Employees, OIP Op. Ltr. No. 90-1 (Jan. 8, 1990).

93. Disclosure of an Individual's Birthdate and Social Security Number, OIP Op. Ltr. No. 90-7 (Feb. 9, 1990).

94. Disclosure of Home Telephone Numbers of Bd. of Water Supply Customers, OIP Op. Ltr. No. 90-9 (Feb. 26, 1990).

95. Disclosure of Certified List of Eligibles and Civil Service Examination Scores, OIP Op. Ltr. No. 90-14 (Mar. 30, 1990); *cf.* Disclosure of Interview Scores and Interview Panelists' Notes Concerning Employment Applicants, OIP Op. Ltr. No. 91-24 (Nov. 26, 1991) (allowing disclosure of aggregate data on applicants' interview scores).

96. Disclosure of Law School Applicant Information, OIP Op. Ltr. No. 95-10 (May 4, 1995).

97. Disclosure of Individuals' Identities in Honolulu City Ethics Comm'n Opinions, OIP Op. Ltr. NO. 96-02 (July 16, 1996).

98. *See* Painting Industry of Haw. Market Recovery Fund v. Alm, 69 Haw. 449, 453-54, 746 P.2d 79, 82 (1987) (refusing to protect, under UIPA's predecessor provisions, records of a settlement agreement between the Department of Commerce and Consumer Affairs and a contractor charged with licensing violations and citing Comm. of the Whole Rep. No. 15, *reprinted in* 1 Proceedings of the Constitutional Convention of Haw. of 1978, at 1024 (1980)).

99. Executive Search Report Pertaining to Special Master for Corrections Sys., OIP Op. Ltr. No. 89-2 (Oct. 27, 1989); *see also* Applications for Appointment to Bds. and Comm'ns, OIP Op. Ltr. No. 91-8 (June 24, 1991) (noting that unsuccessful applications are protected).

100. Disclosure of Hawaiian Home Lands Waiting List, OIP Op. Ltr. No. 89-4 (Nov. 9, 1989).

101. Information Concerning Honolulu Police Dep't Officers, OIP Op. Ltr. No. 91-26 (Dec. 13, 1991) (requiring disclosure of police department sick leave records); *see* Disclosure of Information Relating to the Vacation and Sick Leave of Agnecy Officers and Employees, OIP Op. Ltr. No. 90-17 (Apr. 24, 1990).

102. Public Access to Firearms Registration Information, OIP Op. Ltr. No. 90-25 (July 25, 1990).

103. Disclosure of Sexual Harrassment Complaint and Disciplinary Action Taken Against Univ. of Haw. Faculty Member, OIP Op. Ltr. 90-12 (Feb. 26, 1990), *aff'd* Corollary Issues Regarding OIP Op. Ltr. No. 90-12 (Feb. 26, 1990) Pertaining to Sexual Harrassment Charges, OIP Op. Ltr. No. 90-39 (Dec. 31, 1990) (involving disclosure of sexual harassment complaints filed at the University of Hawaii).

104. Disclosure of the Sanitarian's Final Report Concerning a Food Poisoning Incident, OIP Op. Ltr. No. 91-27, at 1 (Dec. 13, 1991).

105. Public Access to Ambulance Report Form Concerning a Deceased Individual, OIP Op. Ltr. No. 91-33, at 5 (Dec. 31, 1991) (finding ambulance report involving deceased not protected); *see also* Burnham Broad. Co. v. County of Haw. Civ. No. 92-0161 (Haw. 3d Cir. Ct. filed Feb. 14, 1992) (ordering release of 911 tapes concerning rape/murder case); Disclosure of Photograph of Deceased Former Employee, OIP Op. Ltr. 97-2, at 6 (Mar. 11, 1997). *But see* Disclosure of Autopsy Reports, OIP Op. Ltr. No. 91-32, at 12-13 (Dec. 31, 1991) (protecting autopsy report containing information regarding third party until investigation and prosecution had been completed or abandoned).

106. Intra-Agency Memoranda Cited or Identified at a Pub. Meeting, OIP Op. Ltr. No. 91-22, at 1-2 (Nov. 25, 1991) (stating that substantial discussions of a civil rights discrimination claim at an unrelated public hearing waived the government's right to refuse to disclose information thereon).

107. Haw. Rev. Stat. § 92F-13(3) (Supp. 1992).

108. Haw. Sen. Stand. Comm. Rep. No. 2850, 14th Leg., Reg. Sess. (1988), reprinted in 1988 Haw. Senate J. 1093, 1095.

109. Public Access to Aloha Stadium Litig. Settlement Agreements, OIP Op. Ltr. No. 89-10 (Dec. 12, 1989).

110. Drafts of Correspondence and Staff Notes About an Alleged Zoning Violation, OIP Op. Ltr. No. 90-8 (Feb. 26, 1990).

111. Public Inspection of Univ. Program Reviews, OIP Op. Ltr. No. 90-11 (Feb. 26, 1990).

112. Videotaped Recording of Grace Imura-Kotani's Confession, OIP Op. Ltr. No. 90-18 (May 18, 1990).

113. Disclosure of Identities of Complainants to Dep't of Health Alleging Violations of Hawaii Labeling Laws, OIP Op. Ltr. NO. 99-7 (Nov. 23 1999).

114. Disclosure of Identities of Individuals Named in a Criminal Investigation, OIP Op. Ltr. No. 99-9 (Dec. 3, 1999).

115. Confidentiality of Names of Persons Serving on Admissions Comm. for Wm. S. Richardson School of Law, OIP Op. Ltr. No. 89-9 (Nov. 20, 1989).

116. Wm. S. Richardson School of Law Accreditation Reports, OIP Op. Ltr. No. 91-15 (Sept. 10, 1991).

117. Public Inspection of Airport Concessioner Revenue Audits, OIP Op. Ltr. No. 90-3 (Jan. 18, 1990).

118. Public Inspection of Supervisory Management Training Course Materials, OIP Op. Ltr. No. 90-6 (Jan. 31, 1990).

119. Public Inspection of Gov't Contract Lump Sum Bid Price Components, OIP Op. Ltr. No. 90-15 (Apr. 9, 1990).

120. Honolulu Police Dep't Standards of Conduct, OIP Op. Ltr. No. 91-3 (Mar. 22, 1991).

121. Public Access to Police Blotter Information, OIP Op Ltr. No. 91-4 (Mar. 25, 1991).

122. Kaapu v. Aloha Tower Dev. Corp., 74 Haw. 365, 846 P.2d 882 (1993).

123. Kaapu v. Aloha Tower Dev. Corp., 72 Haw. 267, 814 P.2d 396 (1991) (denying standing to employ lis pendens; related case).

124. *Kaapu*, 74 Haw. at 378-79, 846 P.2d at 888.

125. *Id.* at 385-86, 846 P.2d at 891.

126. Applicability of UIPA to Aloha Tower Dev. Proposals, OIP Op. Ltr. No. 89-15 (Dec. 20, 1989).

127. *Kaapu*, 74 Haw. at 385, 846 P.2d at 891.

128. Haw. Rev. Stat. § 92F-13(3) (Supp. 1992).

129. *Kaapu,* 74 Haw. at 390, 846 P.2d at 892.

130. *See, e.g.,* Wm. S. Richardson School of Law Accreditation Reports, OIP Op. Ltr. No. 91-15, at 2, 9-17 (Sept. 10, 1991).

131. *See* 5 U.S.C. § 522b(c)(9) (1977).

132. Haw. Rev. Stat. § 92F-13(4) (1993).

133. *Id.* § 235-116 (1993).

134. *Id.* § 350-1.4 (1993 & Supp. 2002).

135. *Id.* § 338-18.

136. *Id.* § 346-10.

137. *Id.* § 92F-13(5).

138. S.P. No. 6126 (Haw. 1st Cir. 1984), *appeal dismissed,* 67 Haw. 671 (1984).

139. Opening Brief at 3-6, Abercrombie v. Senate, No. 9451 (Haw. filed Dec. 5, 1983), *appeal dismissed,* 67 Haw. 671 (1984).

140. Findings of Fact, Abercrombie v. Senate, S.P. No. 6126 (Haw. 1st Cir. May 23, 1984).

141. Haw. Rev. Stat. §§ 92-50 to 92-52 (1985).

142. Act 262 § 3, 14th Leg., Reg. Sess. (1988), *reprinted in* 1988 Haw. Sess. Laws 473.

143. Unfiled Senate Comm. Report, OIP Op. Ltr. No. 90-19 (May 23, 1990).

144. Haw. Rev. Stat. § 92F-13(2) (1993).

145. DLNR Investigation Report Concerning the Pacific Whale Found., OIP Op. Ltr. No. 91-9 (July 18, 1991) (protecting Department of Land and Natural Resources civil proceedings investigative report).

146. *Id.*

147. SHOPO v. Society of Prof'l Journalists—Univ. of Haw. Chapter, 83 Hawai'i 378, 394-96, 927 P.2d 386, 402-04 (1996).

148. Haw. Rev. Stat. § 92F-19 (1993 & Supp. 2002).

149. *See* DLNR Investigation Report Concerning the Pacific Whale Found., OIP Op. Ltr. 91-9 (July 18, 1991).

150. Inter-Agency Disclosure of Health Fund Membership Lists, OIP Op. Ltr. No. 91-18, at 7 (Oct. 15, 1991).

151. *Id.* at 2 ("confidential information disclosed under section 92F-19, Hawaii Revised Statutes, does not lose its confidential status once it is received by the requesting agency").

152. Haw. Rev. Stat. § 92F-3 (1993).

153. *Id.* § 92F-21.

154. *Id.* § 92F-21.

155. *Id.* § 92F-22.

156. *Id.* § 92F-15(a) (regarding denial of access to a government records); *id.* § 92F-26 (regarding denial of access to a personal record).

157. 5 U.S.C.§ 552 (1994).

158. SHOPO v. Society of Prof'l Journalists—Univ. of Haw. Chapter, 83 Hawai'i 378, 392, 927 P.2d 386, 400 (1996).

159. *Id.* § 92F-15(b).

160. *Id.* § 92F-15.5.

161. *Id.* § 92F-15.5(b).

162. *Id.* § 92F-24.

163. *Id.* § 92F-27.

164. *Id.* § 92F-27.5.

165. *Id.* § 92F-27(a).

166. *Id.* § 92F-23.

167. *Id.*

168. *Id.* § 92F-24(b).

169. *Id.* § 92F-25(a).

170. *Id.* § 92F-24(b)(2).

171. *Id.* § 92F-25(b)(1).

172. *Id.* § 92F-25(b)(2).

173. *Id.* § 92F-17(a).

174. *Id.* § 92F-17(b).

175. *Id.* § 92F-17.

176. *Id.*

177. *Id.* § 92F-16; *see also* Scope of the UIPA's Immunity Provision (Section 92F-16, Haw. Rev. Stat.), OIP Op. Ltr. No. 91-20, at 1 (Oct. 20, 1991) (regarding *Honolulu Advertiser's* request to inspect city records on rapid transit system bidding).

178. Scope of the UIPA's Immunity Provision (Section 92F-16, Haw. Rev. Stat.), OIP Op. Ltr. No. 91-20, at 1 (Oct. 20, 1991).

179. Haw. Rev. Stat. § 92F-27(c)(1) (1993).

180. *Id.*

181. *Id.* § 92F-27(d).

182. Order Granting Plaintiffs All Attorneys' Fees and Costs, Burnham Broad. Co. v. County of Haw., Civ. No. 92-061 (Haw. 3d Cir. Ct. filed June 22, 1992), *see also* Judgment, *Burnham*, (filed July 13, 1992).

Chapter 7
Protecting Information and Sources

Hawaii has no statute defining a newsperson's privilege to refuse to disclose confidential sources(1) nor is such a privilege enumerated in the Hawaii Rules of Evidence.(2) In other words, there is no so-called "shield law" protecting a journalist from having to reveal confidential sources of information. Nevertheless, a qualified privilege arguably exists in Hawaii and is based primarily on federal and state constitutional principles. A recent Hawaii case seems to confirm the existence of a qualified privilege for newspersons while emphasizing that it must be balanced against other constitutionally protected interests.(3)

The seminal federal case in any analysis of journalists' privilege against disclosure of confidential sources is *Branzburg v. Hayes*.(4) In that case, the plurality opinion of the court held that journalists have no First Amendment privilege to preserve the confidentiality of their sources from disclosure before grand juries investigating allegedly criminal conduct.(5) At the same time, however, *Branzburg* acknowledged that the press is protected from official harassment(6) and referred to "occasional dicta that, in circumstances not presented here" might excuse a newsperson from disclosing confidential sources.(7)

Branzburg v. Hayes(8) involved consolidated cases including one concerning the compelled grand jury testimony of a *New York Times* reporter who had infiltrated the Black Panthers.(9) The *Branzburg* plurality opinion stated that freedom of the press does not exempt a newsperson from responding to grand jury subpoenas and investigations.(10) Emphasizing both a public duty to cooperate in law enforcement efforts and the grand jury's function of "protecting citizens against unfounded criminal prosecutions,"(11) four Justices rejected the notion of a conditional privilege that would place the burden of showing necessity on the party seeking disclosure, i.e., a privilege under which a court might require a reporter to disclose confidential sources only after a showing that the information requested was relevant, that another source was unavailable, and that there was a compelling need justifying disclosure.(12)

The Court's opinion noted the difficulty of "predicting in advance when and [under] what circumstances . . . [newspersons] could be compelled to [appear and testify about their sources]...."(13) and explained: "If newsmen's confidential sources are as sensitive as they are claimed to be, the prospect of being unmasked whenever a judge determines the situation justifies it is hardly a satisfactory solution to the problem."(14)

Justice Powell, however, in a brief but important concurring opinion,(15) stated:

> If a newsman believes that the grand jury investigation is not being conducted in good faith he is not without remedy. Indeed, if the newsman is called upon to give information bearing only a remote and tenuous relationship to the subject of the investigation, or if he had some other reason to believe that his testimony implicates confidential source relationships without a legitimate need of law enforcement, he will have access to the Court on a motion to quash and an appropriate protective order may be entered. The asserted claim to privilege should be judged on its facts by the striking of a proper balance between freedom of the press and the obligation of all citizens to give relevant testimony with respect to criminal activity. . . . In short, the courts will be available to newsmen under circumstances where legitimate First Amendment interests require protection.(16)

Powell's *Branzburg* concurrence allows a reporter to challenge a subpoena to testify by asserting a qualified privilege.

His opinion has subsequently been adopted by many state and federal courts.

In a case decided prior to *Branzburg*, the Hawaii Supreme Court, in *In Re Goodfader's Appeal*,(17) a case that had arisen prior to Hawaii's statehood and which therefore called for decision solely on the basis of federal constitutional law,(18) held that a newsperson had no constitutional right to conceal the identity of his sources.(19) The *Goodfader* court employed a balancing test to reach its holding that the necessity for judicial authority over witnesses outweighed any infringement of freedom of the press.(20)

Goodfader was a news reporter who refused to disclose his confidential source for a story involving the dismissal of a government employee who subsequently filed a civil lawsuit contesting her dismissal.(21) The court noted that although First Amendment rights deserve zealous protection they are not absolute.(22) When First Amendment rights and privileges are threatened, courts balance the interests involved.(23) A journalist may be compelled to reveal a source if the public interest in the disclosure needed for judicial fairness outweighs the First Amendment objective to ensure an unfettered press.(24)

Goodfader recognized that "the widest possible dissemination of information from diverse and antagonistic sources is essential to the welfare of the public" and "that a free press is a condition of a free society."(25) Nevertheless, the court ordered Goodfader to disclose his source, noting that the litigants were entitled to judicial assistance in compelling the attendance and testimony of witnesses.(26)

The *Goodfader* majority emphasized that the lack of a newsperson privilege under the facts of the case did not violate the First Amendment guarantee of a free press and that absent statutory provisions (often called shield laws) newspersons do not enjoy special evidentiary privileges.(27) The *Goodfader* majority pointed out that witnesses, whether journalists or members of the general public, have a public duty to support the administration of justice.(28)

Judge Lewis noted in her *Goodfader* concurrence(29) that the newsperson compelled to disclose sources may be "unnecessarily injured by the manner in which the parties are conducting their case."(30) In Judge Lewis' view, the newsperson subpoenaed to disclose confidential sources "is in the position of asserting against [the parties in litigation] that there is a resultant injustice to [the reporter] in the exploration [and discovery of evidence that] they are conducting."(31)

Judge Lewis' concurrence in *Goodfader*(32) stated that a journalist's privilege against disclosure, absent statutory provisions, is subject to a case-by-case review and involves constitutional issues and conflicting interests that must be balanced against each other taking into account the importance of disclosure to the parties seeking access to the reporter's confidential sources.(33) Judge Lewis' *Goodfader* concurrence seemed to presage Justice Powell's concurring opinion in *Branzburg*.

The validity of *Goodfader* today is unclear. In an unreported decision, a Hawaii trial court questioned the applicability of *Goodfader* in light of later federal decisions recognizing the newsperson's privilege.(34) In *Belanger v. City & County of Honolulu*, the court held that a qualified newsperson's privilege barred the plaintiff in a personal injury lawsuit from accessing unpublished photographs of an accident scene taken by a newspaper photographer. On the other hand, a recent Hawaii Supreme Court case, *Jenkins v. Liberty Newspapers Ltd.*,(35) quoted a passage from a U.S. Supreme Court case(36) that in turn cited *Branzburg* for the principle that the First Amendment does not relieve a newsperson of the obligation to respond to subpoenas and cooperate with a criminal investigation, even if that might require revealing a confidential source.(37) Whether this indirect reference to *Branzburg* carries precedential weight, however, is questionable since the newsperson's privilege was not an issue in *Jenkins*.

The *Branzburg*-based limited newspersons' privilege was

directly tested by a Hawaii case involving misdemeanor charges brought by the government against a prominent politician in relation to his business dealings.(38) The district court issued a subpoena to a newspaper reporter, seeking to compel his testimony when he was covering the trial, thereby precluding him from reporting on the trial.(39)

The reporter, before the trial, had published three interviews with the Republican businessman. When subpoenaed to testify at the trial, the reporter refused invoking his First Amendment guarantee of free press and his Fourteenth Amendment Due Process right to pursue his occupation.

The state district court—construing federal case law—held that in Hawaii neither an absolute nor a qualified privilege for news reporters exists.(40) The reporter immediately appealed to the Supreme Court, and in a two-page order the Court quoted Justice Powell's concurrence in *Branzburg*: "The asserted claim to privilege must be decided on a case-by-case basis accord[ing] with the tried and traditional way of adjudicating such questions."(41) Although the state supreme court dismissed the reporter's petition, it refused to hold him in contempt of court for his refusal to testify.(42) Instead, the court indicated that it would review each question posed to the reporter and his response to each to determine whether his refusal to testify constituted contempt.

The businessman subsequently agreed to plead guilty to misdemeanor charges, precluding a conflict over the First Amendment, free press values raised by the reporter's refusal to testify.

Literal readings of the majority holdings in *Goodfader* and the plurality holding of *Branzburg* that preclude the existence of a newpersons' privilege do not appear to be controlling. Rather, it is the concurring opinions of Judge Lewis and Justice Powell, respectively, that provide a constitutional basis for finding that reporters may in some instances successfully assert a privilege against revealing confidential sources in court. To defeat a subpoena requiring them to testify, reporters relying on the privilege must be prepared to show that their interests in concealing such sources have both a constitutional basis and outweigh other interests protected by the state and federal constitutions.

In a case involving the *Maui News*, the trial judge held that a reporter sued by several policemen for libel did not have to immediately reveal his sources until the plaintiffs had first exhausted other opportunities for disclosure and discovery.(43) The court indicated that the person seeking this information would have to demonstrate that the information was not readily available from other sources and was critical to the issues of the case. The case subsequently settled without further hearing on these issues.

The standard of review for reversing a court's ruling to enforce (or quash) a subpoena is extremely high. Such orders will be overturned on appeal only if they are plainly arbitrary and without support in the record.(44)

The case of *DeRoburt v. Gannett Co., Inc.*(45) illustrates another significant limitation on the journalists' privilege. The case shows how assertion of the privilege "may come into conflict with other constitutional values."(46) The *DeRoburt* court determined that media defendants could not use the limited newsperson's privilege, which is based on First Amendment protection of a free press,(47) as a means of concealing their sources from public figure plaintiffs seeking to surmount the standard of actual malice needed to prevail in defamation suits against the media.(48) While holding that compelling reporters to reveal their sources should be "a last resort after pursuit of other opportunities has failed,"(49) the federal district judge presiding over the *DeRoburt* case also held that should the reporter ordered to do so continue to refuse to disclose his or her sources, the court, for purposes of the plaintiff's libel lawsuit, would presume that the media defendant had no source.(50) The court reached its holding after outlining that it was required to and had engaged in a three-part balancing-of-interests inquiry.(51) Under the three-part inquiry applicable to the assertion in civil libel cases of a newsperson's privilege not to testify, the court must determine (1) that the information sought is a "critical element" "going to the heart" of the plaintiff's case, (2) that the plaintiff, by showing that the information sought from the reporter is not otherwise reasonably available, has "demonstrated specific need" for the evidence sought, and (3) that the plainitiff has shown that his claim is not "without merit".(52)

DeRoburt concerned a libel suit filed by the president of Nauru against Gannett Company and its subsidiary in Guam for publication of an article alleging that the president had been involved in illegal loans financed by U.S. aid dollars. The reporter who had written the article refused to reveal the confidential sources for his article. The trial took nearly ten years to reach a final resolution, and only near the end of it did the reporter reveal his sources, one of them by then deceased. A jury found for the defendant newspaper,(53) the plaintiff appealed, and the Ninth Circuit held that the newspaper defendant could not be sanctioned with a holding that no sources existed for its reporter's article, as requested by the plaintiff, notwithstanding the newspaper's reporter's earlier refusal to disclose his sources, because such a holding would be contrary to the truth.(54)

Contempt

Courts can enforce a subpoeanaed witness' duty to testify by holding him or her in contempt of court.(55) This sanction can be applied to journalists.(56) Where intent to avoid the subpoena is shown beyond a reasonable doubt, the sanction is criminal contempt and is punitive in nature.(57) In contrast, civil contempt is concerned only with "whether alleged contemnors have complied with the court's order;" actual compliance is the sole issue, and motive and intent are not at issue.(58)

Unless the court treats an offense charged as criminal contempt as a petty misdemeanor, the defendant is entitled to a jury trial.(59) Jury trial is not a constitutional requirement for criminal contempt when treated as a petty misdemeanor or for civil offenses, including civil contempt.

The court may summarily convict a defendant accused of criminal contempt when the offense is treated as a petty misdemeanor "[i]f the offense was committed in the immediate view and presence of the court."(60) A conviction summarily and instantaneously made by the court for direct criminal contempt—for contempt committed within "the immediate view and presence of the court"—can occur without procedural due process protections, including advance notice of a sentence and an opportunity to be heard(61) and is unappealable.(62) Otherwise, at least in cases of constructive criminal contempt, the defendant may be entitled to advance notice and a hearing before an impartial tribunal, that is, before one presided over by the judge other than the judge lodging the charge.(63)

The court convicting a witness of civil contempt may incarcerate the witness until he or she complies with a court order,(64) including an order to disclose confidential sources.(65) Such instances are rare but have occurred in Hawaii.

Endnotes

1. *See* Haw. Rev. Stat. ch. 626 (1993).
2. *See* Haw. R. Evid. 501 (1985) (codified at Haw. Rev. Stat. ch. 526).
3. State v. Anderson, No. BC00634 (Haw. 1st Cir. Dist. Ct.) (Sept. 24, 1984); *see infra* notes 34-38 and accompanying text.
4. 408 U.S. 665 (1972).
5. *Id.* at 708.
6. *Id.* at 707.
7. *Id.* at 686 (citing In re Goodfader, 45 Haw. 317, 367 P.2d 472 (1961)).
8. 408 U.S. 665 (1972).
9. *Id.* at 711.
10. *Id.* at 708.
11. *Id.* at 685, 686-87.
12. *Id.* at 703-06; *cf. id.* at 740 (Stewart, J., joined by Brennan and Marshall, JJ., dissenting).
13. *Id.* at 702.
14. *Id.*
15. *Id.* at 709-10 (Powell, J., concurring).
16. *Id.* at 710
17. 45 Haw. 317, 367 P.2d 472 (1961).
18. *Id.* at 321 n.2, 367 P.2d at 475 n.2.
19. *Id.* at 327-28, 367 P.2d at 479-80.

20. *Id.* at 329, 367 P.2d at 480.

21. *Id.* at 319, 367 P.2d at 475.

22. *See id.* at 323-25, 367 P.2d at 477-78.

23. *Id.* at 324-25, 367 at 478.

24. *Id.* at 324-25, 367 P.2d at 478.

25. *Id.* at 323-24, 367 P.2d at 477 (quoting Associated Press v. United States, 326 U.S. 1, 20 (1945)).

26. *Id.* at 325, 367 P.2d at 478.

27. *Id.* at 326-30, 367 P.2d at 479-80; *cf. Branzburg*, 408 U.S. 665, 706 (allowing Congress and state legislatures to fashion laws creating a newspersons' privilege and noting inherent power of state courts to so interpret state constitutional provisions).

28. 45 Haw. at 325, 367 P.2d at 478 (quoting Blackmer v. United States, 284 U.S. 421, 438 (1932)).

29. *Id.* at 344-52, 367 P.2d at 487-91.

30. *Id.* at 349, 367 P.2d at 489.

31. *Id.* at 349, 367 P.2d at 490.

32. *Id.* at 344-52, 367 P.2d at 487-91 (Lewis, J., concurring).

33. *Id.* at 351, 367 P.2d at 491.

34. Belanger v. City & County of Honolulu, No. 93-4047-10 (Haw. 1st Cir. Ct. May 4, 1994).

35. 89 Hawai'i 254, 971 P.2d 1089 (1999).

36. Cohen v. Cowles Media Co., 501 U.S. 663 (1991).

37. *Jenkins*, 89 Hawai'i at 262, 971 P.2d at 1097 (citing *Cohen*, 501 U.S. 663).

38. State v. Anderson, No. BC00634 (Haw. 1st Cir. Dist. Ct.) (filed 1984).

39. Motion to Quash Subpoena, State v. Anderson, No. BC00634 (Haw. 1st Cir. Dist. Ct.) (filed Sept. 24, 1984).

40. Order Denying Petition for Writ of Mandamus, State v. Anderson, No. BC00634 (Haw. 1st Cir. Dist. Ct.) (Sept. 24, 1984) (denying writ of mandamus to quash subpoena of reporter to testify).

41. Order Setting Aside Petition, Kato v. Smith, No. 10171 (Sept. 25, 1984) (Lum, C.J.) (order dismissing petition for writ of mandamus to quash subpoena of reporter to testify in State v. Anderson, No. BC00634 (Haw. 1st Cir. Dist. Ct. 1984)).

42. *Id.*

43. Myers v. Maui Publ'g Co., Ltd., Civ. No. 85-0577(3) (Haw. 2d Cir. 1985).

44. Powers v. Shaw, 1 Haw. App. 374, 376, 619 P.2d 1098, 1101 (1980) (upholding quash of subpoena in a property foreclosure case).

45. 507 F. Supp. 880 (D. Haw. 1981) (involving the libel suit brought by the President of Nauru for the publication of articles alleging he secretly made illegal loans to a political commission).

46. *Id.* at 883.

47. *Id.*

48. *Id.* at 884; *see also* ch. 1.

49. *DeRoburt*, 507 F. Supp. at 885.

50. *Id.* at 887.

51. *Id.* at 886.

52. *Id.*; *cf.* Downing v. Monitor Publ'g Co., 415 A.2d 683 (N.H. 1980) (setting forth a similar standard for the imposition of the sanction that a refusal to disclose confidential sources will constitute a presumption that the media defendant had no sources for an allegedly libelous publication concerning a public figure).

53. 859 F.2d 714, 715 (1988), *cert. denied*, 493 U.S. 846.

54. *Id.* at 716.

55. Haw. R. Civ. Pro. 45(f) (1985); Haw. Rev. Stat. § 710-1077(1)(h) (1993).

56. Branzburg v. Hayes, 408 U.S. 665, 684 (1972).

57. Hawaii Pub. Employees Rel. Bd. v. Hawaii State Teachers Ass'n, 55 Haw. 386, 392, 520 P.2d 422, 426 (1974) (adjudicating failure of teachers' union to abide by a court injunction enjoining a strike until the injunction was ruled erroneous); State v. Brown, 70 Haw. 459, 463-64, 776 P.2d 1182, 1185-86 (1989) (refusing to uphold criminal contempt conviction where plaintiff was involved in two trials simultaneously and failed to appear at the continuance of one of them after completing her appearance at the other trial).

58. Hawaii Pub. Employees Rel. Bd. v. Hawaii State Teachers Ass'n, 55 Haw. at 392, 520 P.2d at 427.

59. Haw. Rev. Stat. § 710-1077(3) (1985).

60. *Id.* § 710-1077(3)(a). Criminal contempt committed under such circumstances is known as "direct contempt." *See id.* cmt.

61. Gabriel v. Gabriel, 7 Haw. App. 95, 100 n.5, 746 P.2d 574, 577 n.5 (1987).

62. Haw. Rev. Stat. § 710-1077(5) (1993) (allowing review of a summary or "direct" criminal contempt conviction that has been handled as a petty misdemeanor only by petition for extraordinary writ); *see also In re* Nam, 65 Haw. 119, 648 P.2d 1101 (1982) (upholding the imposition by the presiding judge of a summary punishment of a 24-hour imprisonment of an attorney whose openly contemptuous conduct in court threatened to disrupt the proceedings and refusing a petition for writ of habeas corpus).

63. State v. Brown, 70 Haw. 459, 467-68, 776 P.2d 1182, 1188 (1989).

64. Haw. Rev. Stat. § 710-1077(6) (1993).

65. Farr v. Pitchess, 522 F.2d 464, 469 (9th Cir. 1975), *cert. denied*, 427 U.S. 912 (1976).

Chapter 8

Covering the Courts

Hawaii's Courts

Hawaii, like every state, has two court systems: a federal court system and a state court system. Unlike many other states, however, Hawaii does not have a system of county courts. Both court systems in Hawaii handle both civil and criminal trials. The state court system contains special family, probate, and land courts as well as district courts, which include the traffic court and the small claims courts and which handle claims falling under certain monetary limitations and misdemeanor and petty criminal matters.

The state court system in Hawaii comprises four circuits located on the islands of Oahu (First Circuit); Maui (Second Circuit) including the neighboring islands of Lanai and Molokai; Hawaii— the Big Island (Third Circuit); and Kauai (Fifth Circuit). Each circuit has its own courthouses where trials are conducted. The state circuit courts also act as courts of appeal for adjudicative decisions reached by state administrative agencies and as the state tax appeals court. Decisions of the circuit courts may be appealed to the appellate division of the Hawaii Judiciary, which includes the Hawaii Intermediate Court of Appeals and the Hawaii State Supreme Court.

The federal court system in Hawaii comprises the federal District Court of the District of Hawaii, which includes a bankruptcy court. Hawaii's federal court is part of the Ninth Circuit; appeals of decisions from the federal district court are heard by the Circuit Court of Appeals for the Ninth Circuit.

Fair Trial—Free Press

In court proceedings, particularly those involving criminal charges, a tension often arises between fair trial concerns and free press interests. The Sixth Amendment to the U.S. Constitution,(1) made applicable to the states through the Fourteenth Amendment, requires that states protect a defendant's right to a fair trial.(2) Conflicts arise when the Sixth Amendment guarantee of a fair trial is threatened by the guarantee of a free press embodied in the First Amendment.(3) The tension is most visible when defendants allege that pretrial or trial publicity has prejudiced the fairness of the judicial proceedings against them.(4)

A leading federal case on the issue is *Nebraska Press Association v. Stuart*.(5) In connection with a multiple murder trial, the trial court issued a prior restraint, or gag order, prohibiting any publication or broadcast of confessions or information implicating the accused. The United States Supreme Court reversed the lower court, holding that the trial court's blanket order violated the First Amendment's protection of a free press. The trial judge issuing the gag order had not shown, the Court held, that his order was the only way to prevent a prejudicial result at trial, or that the press was the only source of potentially prejudicial information in a community of roughly 800 people.(6) The Court, discussing the tension between fair trial and free press interests, concluded that there is "a heavy presumption against [the] constitutional validity" of "[a]ny prior restraint on expression."(7)

Hawaii's Constitution has a provision comparable to the Sixth Amendment that guarantees a fair trial to those accused of crimes.(8) The Hawaii provision was intended to incorporate federal court decisions construing the Sixth Amendment.(9) Standing in potential opposition to the defendant's Sixth Amendment rights are the free press protections of the Hawaii Constitution,(10) which afford the media, like the public,(11) a right of access to criminal proceedings.(12)

In Hawaii, as elsewhere, the media's right of access to judicial proceedings is not absolute. It is subject to a balancing of the public's free press interests against the individual defendant's right to due process.(13) If the influence of the news media clearly interferes with the court proceedings, the court may conclude that unfairness to the defendant may result.(14) Absent such a situation, the defendant bears an affirmative burden to show that essential unfairness resulted from a demonstrable reality that he or she did not receive a fair trial because of prejudicial pretrial publicity.(15) Furthermore, the media's constitutionally protected right to report on court proceedings is not infringed upon if a judge's orders impose merely "incidental burdens" on news gathering capabilities.(16)

The case of *Advertiser v. Takao* involved a trial judge's order to seal a court reporter's transcript of preliminary hearings in a controversial rape/sodomy trial. Noting that court reporters, as officers of the court, are "subject to orders of the presiding judge,"(17) the Hawaii Supreme Court held that the media's right of access to the reporter's transcript or to her shorthand notes was not absolute and that it certainly was no greater than that of the public.(18)

The court stated that access to court proceedings, particularly those that create unfair pretrial publicity and the potential prejudice resulting therefrom, are, within certain standards, left to the discretion of the trial judge.(19) It declined to adopt the media's argument that the court reporter's transcript be released from the district court judge's protective order placing it under seal.(20)

However, in *Gannett Pacific Corp. v. Richardson*, decided on the same day as *Takao*, the Hawaii Supreme Court held that in order for the district court to close the preliminary proceedings in a criminal trial to the public, thereby excluding the media as well, the court must have a sufficient basis for its order.(21) In determining whether the public and media could be precluded from court proceedings in which material that might be admissible in a preliminary proceeding on the issue of probable cause but which would not be admissible at trial is to be produced or discussed, the *Richardson* court stated that the trial court judge must consider whether there is a likelihood of prejudice to the defendant from the revelation of such material. The court directed that the judge should consider:

> the nature of the evidence sought to be presented; the
> probability of such information reaching potential

jurors; the likely prejudicial impact of this information upon prospective veniremen; and the availability and efficacy of alternative means to neutralize the effect of such disclosures.(22)

The court continued:

> [B]ecause of our natural suspicion and traditional aversion as a people to secret proceedings, suggestions of unfairness, discrimination, undue leniency, favoritism, and incompetence are more easily entertained when access by the public to judicial proceedings are unduly restricted. ... Thus, the openness which serves as a safeguard against attempts to employ our courts as instruments of persecution also serves to enhance public trust and confidence in the integrity of the judicial process.(23)

These cases, however, were decided two years before the United States Supreme Court expanded the media's and the public's right to attend judicial proceedings in the case of *Richmond Newspapers, Inc. v. Virginia*.(24) The decision enuciated the Court's emphasis on the constitutional right implicit in the First Amendment(25) of the public's right to attend trials(26) and emphasized that, particularly during a trial, as opposed to during preliminary hearings, alternative means of guarding the defendant's Sixth Amendment rights exist. The Court noted that witnesses could be sequestered or excluded from the courtroom and that jurors could be sequestered during certain motions regarding evidence.(27) The Court's opinion, in reversing the lower court's decision to uphold the trial judge's closure of the trial, noted that the Sixth Amendment guarantees criminal defendants a right to a public trial, that "in the context of the trial itself [there exist] various tested alternatives to satisfy the constitutional demands of fairness," and stressed the importance of the "right under the Constitution for the public [and] press to attend the trial."(28) It concluded that a court seeking to issue a valid order constraining or prohibiting media coverage of judicial proceedings court must (1) articulate reasonable grounds for its free press limitation, and (2) use the least restrictive means available to protect the defendant's interests.(29)

The Hawaii Supreme Court subsequently enunciated a similar standard in *Advertiser v. Tsukiyama*,(30) a case in which a circuit court judge had imposed a total ban on media coverage of a controversial criminal trial. Invoking its supervisory jurisdiction,(31) the Supreme Court issued an order lifting the bar to media coverage of the trial "without prejudice to the issuance of any subsequent order by the trial court supported by a written statement of reasons [adequately] described . . . ."(32)

Other alternatives to placing prior restraints on the media include such measures as a continuance of trial to allow media attention to cool,(33) or a change of venue or extensive voir dire to screen out jurors potentially prejudiced by pretrial or even trial publicity.(34) The amount of voir dire needed to assess whether prejudice exists on account of the pretrial publicity will vary from case to case; it is within the trial judge's discretion to determine the length of voir dire.(35)

In the first of two widely publicized criminal trials involving Stephanie Stearns, the defendant initially failed in her efforts to obtain a prior restraint on press coverage.(36) After failing twice before two different judges, Stearns' attorney successfully moved to have the venue for her murder trial transferred to San Francisco.(37) The judge granting the motion cited the widespread publicity devoted to the theft trials in Honolulu,(38) and noted, "[T]he likelihood of prejudice to the defendants and the attendant probability of an unfair trial in the District of Hawaii far outweigh any inconveniences that a change of venue would cause this court or the prosecution."(39) This is the only time in recent Hawaii jurisprudence that a change of venue has been granted. Obviously, in a small island state like Hawaii, an out-of-state change of venue will be quite costly and inconvenient to the parties, witnesses, and the court.

Court Decorum: Conduct, Cameras, Canon 3

Media access may be limited not only by constitutional considerations, but also by the need to maintain solemnity in proceedings and respect for the court itself.

General Conduct

Canon 3 of the Hawaii Judicial Conduct Canons mandates that judges maintain order and decorum in court proceedings.(40) A judge's adjudicative responsibilities further require him to "be patient, dignified and courteous to litigants, jurors, witnesses, lawyers and others with whom he deals in his official capacity."(41) In turn, judges can expect and require similar conduct of persons "subject to his direction and control."(42) In disposing of the court's business, judges and court personnel are restrained from commenting publicly on pending or impending proceedings.(43) However, judges are not similarly prohibited if public statements are made "in the course of their official duties or from explaining for public information the procedures of the court."(44)

Broadcasting Court Proceedings

Photography and audio and video recording are prohibited in the federal district courtrooms in Hawaii.(45) Hawaii is not among the federal court districts authorized to experiment with policies and rules allowing cameras.

In contrast, cameras are allowed in the state courts, subject to important restrictions. In 1979, the Chief Justice of the Hawaii Supreme Court reviewed the then-existing rules governing broadcast media coverage in the courtroom.(46) At that time, the broadcast media were permitted to televise arguments before appellate courts but no cameras or audio recording were permitted in the state's trial courts. In response to media and public pressure to open Hawaii courtrooms to cameras, the Chief Justice determined that guidelines giving "full weight to First and Sixth Amendment considerations, to individual rights of privacy, to the administrative needs of the courtroom and to the technical requirements and limitations of the broadcast equipment itself" were needed.(47) After a three-year experiment, the Hawaii Supreme Court promulgated rules (the Hawaii Rule) governing the use of broadcast media personnel and equipment in State courtrooms.

Hawaii Supreme Court Rule 5.1

General Provisions

This acknowledges the media's right to report on court proceedings(48) and the power of the judge to control the conduct of parties to court proceedings.(49) The Rule generally permits video and audio coverage of court proceedings under rules and guidelines established by the Supreme Court. The media must not "be distracting . . . [nor] interfere with the solemnity, decorum, and dignity which must attend the making of decisions that affect the life, liberty, or property of citizens."(50)

If the media desires to photograph or record a particular court proceeding, they must make a request for extended coverage(51) to the State Judiciary's Office of Public Affairs.(52) An application for extended coverage relates to an entire case, through the final judgment, post-judgment motions, and appeals.(53) A written request is deemed to have been made by all the media.(54) Thus, only one written request per case is necessary.

Except for appellate arguments, extended coverage of all other proceedings is allowed only with prior consent of the judge.(55) A judge may deny a request(56) or terminate or limit extended coverage(57) if good cause is found by a preponderance of the evidence. There is a presumption that good cause exists if:

(1) the proceeding is for the purpose of determining the admissibility of evidence;

(2) testimony regarding trade secrets is being received;

(3) testimony of child witnesses is being received;

(4) testimony of a complaining witness in a prosecution for any sexual offense under Part V of the Hawaii Penal Code is being received;

(5) a witness would be put in substantial jeopardy of serious bodily injury;

(6) testimony of undercover law enforcement agents who are involved in other ongoing undercover investigations is being received.(58)

Further, extended coverage is not allowed:
(1) if the proceedings are closed by law or by the judge;(59)
(2) of jurors or prospective jurors;(60)
(3) of conferences between attorney and client, co-counsel and client or parties, or counsel and judge held at the bench;(61) and
(4) of conferences or proceedings in a judge's chambers.(62)

If these rules are violated, a judge may "limit or terminate extended coverage as to the offending ... personnel or equipment."(63)

Equipment and Personnel Limitations

Rule 5.2 limits the number and type of media personnel and equipment allowed in the courtroom at any one time.(64) The media, by way of a pooling arrangement,(65) are limited to one portable electronic camera operated by one camera person. However, a second camera for live coverage is allowed at the judge's discretion.(66)

Only one audio system for extended coverage is allowed in the courtroom.(67) The media must use the existing audio system unless it is unsuitable. Changes to the system must be approved by the judge, and changes cannot be made at public expense.(68)

Only one still photographer is allowed in the courtroom under the Hawaii Rule; however, a judge may at his discretion approve the presence of a second photographer.(69) A photographer may have up to two still cameras with no more than two lenses per camera.(70)

Equipment used to cover proceedings may not produce distracting sound or light.(71) The use of artificial light with television or still cameras is prohibited.(72)

The insignia or identification of the media is not allowed on the equipment or clothing of extended coverage personnel.(73) Video and audio tape changes should occur during court recesses.(74)

Trial Publicity

In an island community such as Hawaii, it is easy to argue that in certain instances media coverage of trial proceedings might completely undercut the defendant's constitutional guarantee of a fair trial.(75) Hawaii courts have only infrequently considered whether news coverage of trials should be banned altogether because it might, in particular instances, give rise to possible prejudice in the jury proceedings.

When it has considered such issues, the state supreme court—at least as far as resulting outcomes, if not always explicitly in the words of its opinions—has tended to support media coverage.(76)

In one of its most recent cases touching on the issue of trial publicity, the Hawaii Supreme Court, in response to a petition for writ of prohibition, overruled a circuit judge's ban on communications between criminal defendants and the media.(77) Hawaii's ACLU, on behalf of a pro se defendant charged, in the underlying case, with murder of his infant son, asserted that the circuit court judge's gag order failed to show convincingly that conduct threatening jury impartiality actually necessitated the order.(78)

The supreme court agreed by requiring that such orders restraining attorneys from speaking to the media be narrowly drawn as the least restrictive means to prevent threatened, imminent, and serious publicity from endangering the defendant's right to a fair trial.(79)

In fact, in Hawaii there has never (yet) been a criminal conviction reversed because of alleged pretrial publicity.(80) In one case to date, however, the Intermediate Court of Appeals observed that the defendant's appellate counsel's failure to raise on appeal the issue of whether the trial court's denial of the defendant's pro se motion for voir dire of the jury had failed to adequately guard against prejudice resulting from pretrial publicity would not have altered the trial's outcome; because the fairness of the defendant's conviction had been addressed through other issues, the court found that the defendant had not been denied effective assistance of counsel.(81)

Access to Court Records

As a general rule, the public has access to the judicial record in a case unless a protective order barring disclosure of the record is entered upon a showing of "good cause."(82) The party seeking to restrict access has the burden of establishing "good cause" by showing that specific prejudice or harm will result if no protective order is granted.(83)

In addition, the U.S. Supreme Court has recognized a "general right to inspect and copy public records and documents, including judicial records and documents."(84) This federal common law right creates a presumption in favor of access(85) that can be overcome only by showing "sufficiently important countervailing interests."(86) The factors relevant to determine whether the presumption of access is overcome include the public interest in understanding the judicial process and whether disclosure of materials in the judicial record would result in improper use of the materials.(87) However, the presumption of access does not apply to documents filed under seal pursuant to a valid protective order(88) unless it was a "blanket stipulated protective order" entered by the court without a specific finding of good cause with respect to each sealed document.(89)

In a recent federal district court case, the *Honolulu*

Advertiser sought access to sealed court records in a case involving allegations of corruption and misconduct in the Honolulu Police Department.(90) The court had entered a blanket stipulated protective order and sealed significant portions of the record in the case.(91) Ruling on a motion brought by the *Advertiser* to modify the protective order, the court determined that the record was sealed without specific findings of good cause.(92) The court ordered the parties to make a specific showing of good cause as to each document they wanted to keep sealed.(93)

The public is also presumed to have a right to public access to court records under the First Amendment.(94) The presumption can be overcome only if certain procedural and substantive requirements are satisfied. The procedural requirements require a court to afford those denied access a reasonable opportunity to state their objections, and state why it is denying access.(95) Under the substantive requirements, the court must find the following before sealing the record: (1) sealing serves a compelling interest; (2) there is a substantial probability that, in the absence of sealing, this compelling interest would be harmed; and (3) there are no alternatives to sealing that would adequately protect the compelling interest at issue."(96)

Other provisions of state law may also control access to judicial records. For example, the recent case of *Kema v. Gaddis*(97) involved restriction of access to family court records under Hawaii's Child Protective Act.(98) In *Kema*, the *Honolulu Advertiser* requested the family court to release confidential files relating to Peter "Peter Boy" Kema, Jr.—a missing child—and his siblings.(99) The *Advertiser* argued that allowing the media access to the files would serve a legitimate purpose of advancing and protecting the welfare of Peter Boy.(100) The family court released redacted versions of the file relating to Peter Boy, but denied access to the files relating to his siblings.(101) Peter Boy's family successfully obtained a writ of mandamus from the Hawaii Supreme Court prohibiting the family court from releasing the confidential records of Peter Boy's case.(102) The Hawaii Supreme Court reasoned that release of the records would not be in the best interests of the child, which, under the Child Protective Act, are considered more compelling than the interests of other persons seeking information.(103)

Endnotes

1. U.S. Const. amend VI. The amendment reads, in pertinent part: "In all criminal prosecutions, the accused shall enjoy the right to a speedy and public trial, by an impartial jury . . . ." *Id.*
2. State v. Pokini, 55 Haw. 640, 526 P.2d 94 (1974).
3. The First Amendment free press provision—nearly identical to that in the Hawaii Constitution—reads, in pertinent part: "Congress shall make no law . . . abridging the freedom . . . of the press." U.S. Const. amend. I.
4. *See, e.g.*, State v. Wahinekona, 53 Haw. 574, 499 P.2d 678 (1972) (attempting unsuccessfully to argue that the publicity accorded his codefendant's first-degree murder and robbery trial denied the appellant an opportunity for a fair trial on the same charges).
5. 427 U.S. 539 (1976).
6. *Id.* at 563-68.
7. *Id.* at 558.
8. Haw. Const. art. I, § 14. The provision states in pertinent part, "[T]he accused shall enjoy the right to a speedy and *public* trial. . . ." *Id.* (emphasis added).
9. State v. Wong, 47 Haw. 361, 385, 389 P.2d 439, 452 (1964) (citing 1 Proceedings of the Constitutional Convention of Hawaii of 1950, at 164, 302 (1961)).
10. Haw. Const. art. I, § 4 reads, in pertinent part, "No law shall be enacted . . . abridging the freedom . . . of the press."
11. *See* Gannett Pac. Corp. v. Richardson, 59 Haw. 224, 227, 580 P.2d 49, 53 (1978) (setting aside a state district court judge's attempted expulsion of the press from already-commenced preliminary proceedings in a case involving criminal charges).
12. *Id.* at 228, 580 P.2d at 53-54.
13. State v. Wahinekona, 53 Haw. 574, 579, 499 P.2d 678, 682 (1974) (requiring judge to take affirmative steps to avoid prejudice to a defendant when pretrial publicity threatens the ability to hold a fair trial).
14. State v. Graham, 70 Haw. 627, 637, 780 P.2d 1103, 1109 (1989) (failing, however, to find pervasive pretrial publicity prejudicing the defendant's right in a drug trafficking trial to a fair trial).

15. *Id.*

16. Advertiser v. Takao, 59 Haw. 237, 238, 580 P.2d 58, 61 (1978) (sealing transcript upheld on statutory grounds).

17. *Id.* at 239, 580 P.2d at 61.

18. *Id.*

19. *Id.* at 239, 580 P.2d at 62 (citing Nixon v. Warner Comm., Inc., 435 U.S. 589 (1978)).

20. *Id.* at 580 P.2d at 63 (holding that public's "right to be concerned . . . about the growing incidence of crime" must be balanced against the public's responsibility to "continually guard against the erosion of fundamental rights, prominent among which is the right to a fair trial").

21. 59 Haw. 224, 236, 580 P.2d 49, 58 (1978).

22. *Id.* at 233-34, 580 P.2d at 57.

23. *Id.* at 230, 580 P.2d at 55.

24. 448 U.S. 555 (1980).

25. *Id.* at 580.

26. *Id.*

27. *Id.* at 581.

28. *Id.* at 580-81.

29. *See* Order Granting Petition for Writ of Mandamus, Advertiser v. Tsukiyama, Civ. No. 9938 (Haw. 1st Cir. June 7, 1984) (following *Richmond Newspapers*).

30. *Tsukiyama*, Civ. No. 9938 (Haw. 1st Cir. 1984).

31. Haw. Rev. Stat. § 602-4 (1985).

32. Order Granting Petition for Writ of Mandamus, at 2, Advertiser v. Tsukiyama, Civ. No. 9938 (Haw. 1st Cir. Ct. June 7, 1984).

33. State v. Graham, 70 Haw. 626, 636, 780 P.2d 1103, 1109 (1989) (noting that a motion for a continuance seeking to put off a trial involving drug trafficking charges "until the passage of time [had] dissipated the high potential for prejudice" was "hardly a matter of discretion" given the constitutional dimension of the defendant's request for a fair trial).

34. *See, e.g.*, State v. Wahinekona, 53 Haw. 574, 580 n.5, 499 P.2d 678, 682 n.5 (1972) (holding that extensive voir dire, which was instituted by the court after the defendant had made a motion for a continuance of the trial or in the alternative a change of venue, adequately protected the defendant against potential prejudice allegedly stemming from pretrial publicity); State v. LeVasseur, 1 Haw. App. 19, 22-23, 613 P.2d 1328, 1331-32 (1980) (denying a reversal of the defendant's conviction for theft allegedly stemming from prejudicial effects on jurors of pretrial publicity surrounding the fact that the defendant had freed two dolphins from a university research facility).

35. *Id.*

36. Order Denying Motion for Preliminary Injunction (Nov. 27, 1974), Stearns

v. Honolulu Advertiser, Civ. No. 74-275 (D. Haw. 1974).

37. Vincent Bugliosi with Bruce B. Henderson, *And the Sea Will Tell* 201 (1991) (recounting the Stearns/Walker theft and murder trials as told by Stearns' attorney for her murder trial).

38. One survey reported that more than 95% of Honolulu residents thought Stearns and Walker were guilty of the murder. *Id.* at 193 (describing evidence presented in support of initial motion for change of venue, denied).

39. *Id.* at 201 (quoting Order Granting Change of Venue (Aug. 8, 1984)).

40. Haw. Code of Judicial Conduct Canon 3(B)(3) (amended 1992).

41. *Id.* canon 3(B)(4).

42. *Id.*

43. *Id.* canon 3(B)(9).

44. *Id.*

45. U.S. Dist. Ct., Dist. of Haw. R. 83.8.

46. Chief Justice William S. Richardson, Address at Hilo Press Club, *reprinted in Final Report of the Hawaii State Bar Association Committee on "Cameras in the Courtroom"*, 17 Haw. B.J. 4 (1982).

47. *Id.*

48. Haw. Sup. Ct. R. 5.1(d)(1) (amended 1997).

49. *Id.* rule 5.1(d)(4).

50. *Id.* rule 5.1(h)(1).

51. "'Extended coverage' means any recording or broadcasting of proceedings through the use of television, radio, photographic, or recording equipment by the media or on behalf of educational institutions." *Id.* rule 5.1(c)(2).

52. *Id.* rule 5.1(e)(1).

53. *Id.* rule 5.1(e)(2) (amended Sept. 28, 1990).

54. *Id.* rule 5.1(e)(4).

55. *Id.* rule 5.1(f)(1).

56. *Id.* rule 5.1(f)(3).

57. *Id.* rule 5.1(f)(6).

58. *Id.* rule 5.1(f)(5).

59. *Id.* rule 5.1(g)(1).

60. *Id.* rule 5.1(g)(2).

61. *Id.* rule 5.1(g)(3).

62. *Id.* rule 5.1(g)(4).

63. *Id.* rule 5.1(h)(2).

64. *Id.* rule 5.2(a)(1).

65. *See id.* rule 5.1(c)(14).

66. *Id.* rule 5.2(a)(1).

67. *Id.* rule 5.2(a)(2).

68. *Id.*

69. *Id.* rule 5.2(a)(3).

70. *Id.*
71. *Id.* rule 5.2(b).
72. *Id.*
73. *Id.* rule 5.2(a)(4).
74. *Id.* rule 5.2(a)(5).
75. Haw. Const. art. I, § 14 provides in pertinent part, "In all criminal proceedings, the accused shall enjoy a right to a speedy and public trial by an impartial jury of the district wherein the crime shall have been committed . . . or of such other district to which the prosecution may be removed with the consent of the accused . . . ."
76. Advertiser v. Richardson, 59 Haw. 224, 580 P.2d 49 (1978) (barring ban on media coverage of criminal trial being conducted amid heightened public protest over the judge in the case, the Chief Justice's brother); *see also* Advertiser v. Tsukiyama, Civ. No. 9938 (Haw. June 7, 1984).
77. Order Granting Petition for Writ of Prohibition (No. 16152) (Sept. 3, 1992), Breiner v. Takao, 73 Haw. 499, 835 P.2d 637, 639 (1992)
78. Brief of Petitioner (ACLU for Breiner) at 3-4, Breiner v. Takao, 73 Haw. 499, 835 P.2d 637 (1992).
79. *Breiner,* 73 Haw. at 505-07, 835 P.2d at 641-42.
80. *See, e.g.,* State v. Graham, 70 Haw. 627, 780 P.2d 1103 (1989); State v. LeVasseur, 1 Haw. App. 19, 613 P.2d 1328 (1980).
81. State v. Bryant, 6 Haw. App. 331, 340, 720 P.2d 1015, 1020 (1986) (holding that lower court did not abuse its discretion in determining that the extent of pretrial publicity was insufficient to warrant voir dire and that failure to raise the issue on initial appeal did not create "a reasonable probability of reversal or [of] an order for a new trial").
82. *See* Fed. R. Civ. P. 26(c); Phillips v. General Motors Corp., 289 F.3d 1117, 1121 (9th Cir. 2002).
83. *Phillips,* 289 F.3d at 1121.
84. Nixon v. Warner Comm., Inc., 435 U.S. 589, 597 (1978) (footnote omitted).
85. Hagestad v. Tragesser, 49 F.3d 1430, 1434 (9th Cir. 1995).
86. San Jose Mercury News, Inc. v. United States Dist. Ct., 187 F.3d 1096, 1102 (9th Cir. 1999).
87. *Hagestad,* 49 F.3d at 1434.
88. *Phillips,* 289 F.3d at 1121.
89. Beckman Indus., Inc. v. International Ins. Co., 966 F.2d 470, 476 (9th Cir. 1992).
90. Kamakana v. City & County of Honolulu, Civ. No. 00-00729 SOM LEK (D. Haw. Nov. 9, 2000).
91. First Amended Stipulated Protective Order (filed June 1, 2001), Kamakana v. City & County of Honolulu, Civ. No. 00-00729 SOM LEK (D. Haw. Nov. 9, 2000).

92. Order Granting Intervenor Gannett Pacific Corporation, dba The Honolulu Advertiser's Motion to Intervene, Order Granting Intervenor's Motion to Modify Protective Order and Unseal Judicial Record (filed Nov. 25, 2002), at 8, Kamakana v. City & County of Honolulu, Civ. No. 00-00729 SOM LEK (D. Haw. Nov. 9, 2000).

93. *Id.* at 9-10.

94. Press-Enterprise Co. v. Superior Ct., 478 U.S. 1, 8 (1986).

95. Crowe v. County of San Diego, 210 F. Supp. 2d 1189, 1198 (S.D. Cal. 2002) (citing Oregonian Publ'g Co. v. United States Dist. Ct., 920 F.2d 1462, 1466 (9th Cir. 1990)).

96. *Id.* (citing Phoenix Newspapers, Inc. v. United States Dist. Ct., 156 F.3d 940, 949 (9th Cir. 1998)).

97. 91 Hawai'i 200, 982 P.2d 334 (1999).

98. Haw. Rev. Stat. ch. 587; *see id.* § 587-81 (providing that records of child protective proceedings "may be made available to other appropriate persons, who are not parties, only upon order of the court after the court has determined that such access is in the best interest of the child or serves some other legitimate purpose . . . .").

99. *Kema,* 91 Hawai'i at 203, 982 P.2d at 337.

100. *Id.*

101. *Id.* at 203-04, 982 P.2d at 337-38.

102. *Id.* at 204, 206, 982 P.2d at 338, 340.

103. *Id.* at 205, 982 P.2d at 339.